Men of the World

A play

John Godber

Samuel French — London
New York - Toronto - Hollywood

MEN OF THE WORLD

First performed at the Lyceum Theatre, Sheffield, in September 2002, with the following cast:

Frank	Sarah Parks
Stick	Rob Angell
Larry	Dicken Ashworth

Directed by **John Godber**
Designed by **Pip Leckonby**

COPYRIGHT INFORMATION

(See also page ii)

CHARACTERS

Larry, ageing coach driver
Frank, middle-aged female driver
Stick, middle-aged driver

Who also play:

Sissy, lady, 79
Doris, old lady, 80
Jean, ill lady, 79
Wally, retired miner, 68
Len, retired miner, 70
Brian, retired miner, 67
Harry, retired miner, 72
Dot, recovering from heart surgery, 72
Martin, middle-aged man
May, Martin's mum, 63
Mollie, posh ex shop owner
Connie, posh ex shop owner
Raymond, gay bell boy
Clive, gay bell boy
Dolly, club act

Other plays by John Godber
published by Samuel French Ltd:

April in Paris
Blood Sweat and Tears
Departures
Gym and Tonic
Happy Families
It Started With a Kiss
Lucky Sods
Passion Killers
Perfect Pitch
Salt of the Earth
Teechers
Unleashed
Up 'n' Under
Up 'n' Under II
Weekend Breaks

ACT I

A large box set, which has the suggestion of a skyline about it. There are two doors US. The flatage is all treated with the same image. Under the image is a suggestion of the route map of Europe; place names, however, are faintly indicated, and the motorway system is lightly suggested. The stage is littered with suitcases, and in places they are covered with overcoats

Music

Frank enters; she is a striking woman in her mid forties. She carries two large cases on to the stage. As she places the cases C she speaks directly and frankly to the audience

Frank Mystery trip! You'd think they were going round the world. Look at this lot! It's only a one nighter in Scarborough! Everybody on the coach knows that. I mean that's not much of a mystery, is it? This one woman from Howden phoned up and asked where the mystery trip was going; she wouldn't book until Dennis had told her!

Stick enters, a lean nasty-looking but able man, also in his mid forties. He dumps two cases C

Stick Bastards!

Stick turns about face and instantly exits

Frank That's Stick; he doesn't say a lot doesn't Stick, but he's all there. He hates these crinkly trips, I think that's why Dennis puts him on 'em. Just to wind him up. His mate Johnny Mac usually gets the Spanish run, that's what Stick wants, full of sixteen-year-olds and unmarried mothers. He's a right 'un for that is Stick!

Larry enters. He is carrying two cases and a bag under one arm. He is smoking, and already sweating

Larry Nearly there, Frank... (*He dumps his cases and stands and has a long drag on his cigarette*)

Frank That's Larry. Happy Larry they call him … don't know why! I think it's because he's such a grumpy old sod. He's been on the trips for as long as anybody can remember. Used to work for t' Ideal in Pontefract; did the schools run. Nobody messes with Larry, they reckon he used to be in the SAS or sommat, I think that was just a myth he created so people keep their distance.

Larry (*drawing on his cigarette*) Mmm…

Frank He's got a weakness has Larry … he loves Mario Lanza. If he was in the SAS he must have been in the operatic division if they had one, they reckon he could have been a singer or sommat. What that bloke doesn't know about Mario isn't worth knowing… He's not a bad bloke isn't Larry for a man who thinks he's the Red Shadow!

Larry (*drawing on his cigarette again*) Lovely… (*To Frank*) Nearly there… (*He goes for some more cases*)

Frank Nearly there? That's what they ought to call him, he's forever saying it!

Larry (*going*) Nearly there…

Larry exits

Frank The firm's called Larards now, if you're thinking of booking. Formerly Omega Travel, formerly East Coach Travel; formerly Dennis's of Witham. Formerly Dennis's. Oh, and I'm Frank by the way … don't ask; it'll only shock you! I did five years in the Navy, amongst other things, training in everything and qualifying as nowt.

Stick enters carrying a few more cases. He dumps them

Stick What have they got in here?

Frank But it's just a job, isn't it, like owt else. And there's a hundred and one stories! Some get to you … some don't…

Stick (*with the cases*) What do they think we are?

Frank There was that trip to Prague where that bloke went missing in Brussels … wasn't there, Stick?

Stick What?

Frank That bachelor trip to Prague when a bloke went missing.

Stick That was on my bloody run that was! They reckon that he was a spy or sommat.

Frank He wasn't though, was he?

Stick Was he bollocks, he worked for a rubber firm in Rotherham by all accounts.

Frank He drops on does Stick, what about that one you had going to Amsterdam?

Stick Well, she died getting on the bloody ferry.

Frank He gets all the good 'uns!

Stick Didn't know what to do with her. So they stuck her in the lift and brought her back down into the check-in ... lift doors open and there we are holding her; who's stood there waiting for the lift? It's only her sister and she was eighty-two. I think she had a heart do! They buried them both together.

Frank Hey, I've seen women in their sixties struggle to get on here, and have the time of their life in Paris, acting like they're Zsa Zsa Gabor or somebody ... and I'll tell you what ... good luck to 'em!

Stick Age, that's one thing about it!

Frank It's funny because sommat happens on every trip ... look at the last one... A week down the Rhine valley.

Stick Little people...

Frank That's what he calls 'em...

Stick People with nowt...!

Frank Just looking for a cheap holiday...

Stick A load of sad bastards if you ask me, but if that's how they want to spend their money.

Frank They pay your wages...

Stick They should be shot, I think!

Frank He doesn't' mean that.

Stick I do... You've got to do everything for them. They do nowt but complain, in the warm weather they smell ... no, they do! They bore you senseless singing all the way to bloody Dover. It's like being in the *Good Old Days*. They're right bloody moaners on that Rhine Valley trip. That's what Dennis ought to advertise it as. "Five Days Moaning in Germany". Comes a point when you say enough is enough. Seventy-three or seventy-four, shoot 'em!

Frank You'd have to shoot half the House of Lords.

Stick You should shoot them first.

Frank That was supposed to be Larry's last trip.

Stick They should shoot him and all...

Larry enters with another pair of cases. He dumps them US

Larry Nearly there, Stick.

Frank Three days in Heidelberg, with a performance of *The Student Prince* thrown in, wasn't it, Larry?

Larry That's my idea of a good trip that is! Not farting about, going on a mystery trip.

Stick I'd like to take 'em on a mystery trip. Take 'em to Dover and don't stop! Straight over the cliffs ... that'd be a bloody mystery for 'em!

Larry Oh ay, it was a good trip was that ... nice people ... they had some
bloody taste. There was some nice people on that trip; Dot and Harry from
Pontefract were good. I liked them a lot. Mack and Mabel, I called them
two! And what about them three old lads from Donny?

Frank Wally, Len and Brian, ex-miners!

Larry Marx brothers! I called them. That Wally were good, nowt was done
right for him!

Stick Bloody complainers all of 'em...

Larry Who else was there?

Frank Sissy, Jean and Doris from Beverley!

Larry The Beverley Sisters...

Frank And who else...?

Stick That kid with his mam and dad...

Frank Martin!

Stick He was older than me! On a trip with his mam and dad? He had a piece
of pie missing he did!

Larry Seven Brides for Seven Brothers. Desperate for it, wasn't he?

Stick He got it and all; more than I can say for some!

Frank There was them two from Sheffield whose shop had gone bust. Molly
and Connie.

Stick Lesbians they were!

Larry Arsenic and Old Lace!

Frank Ay, it was a good laugh!

Stick It was just another trip...

Larry (*remembering*) It was a good trip was that. I did a lot of thinking on
that trip.

Stick That'd be a bloody first then!

Frank We were late getting to the first pick-up, weren't we?

Larry He was arguing the toss with Dennis about that Spanish trip...

Stick Ay, I can remember 'em... There was Sissy who only had one lung and
was still smoking herself senseless, and the other two sad sods hanging on
to her every bloody word...

Musical sting

The Lights change to slight focus on the DS *area. Frank, Stick and Larry don
headscarves and handbags. They may wear some of the overcoats which are
amongst the cases. They become three old women. Frank plays Sissy. Stick
plays Jean and Larry plays Doris. They are waiting for the Larards coach to
arrive. Sissy smokes. The other two cluck and look around as the music fades
under*

Sissy Late...!

Doris Mmmm...
Jean Twenty minutes...
Doris Mmmm...
Jean My feet are swelling... I've been on 'em that long!
Sissy Wallace Arnold are never late...
Doris No...
Jean No! They're never late them...
Sissy Never late are Wallace Arnold!
Doris No they're not, are they?
Jean Well, I've never known 'em be late.
Sissy These are late though...
Jean Twenty minutes now!
Doris It's a stop-over in Folkestone, then?
Sissy Stop-over in Folkestone...
Jean I went to Folkestone once with Earl...
Sissy Yeah!
Jean Didn't like it...
Sissy No...!
Doris Well, it's only one night, isn't it?
Sissy They're late, aren't they?
Jean (*as if it's just come to mind*) They are, aren't they?
Sissy Mind you, as my Tom used to say. As you get older you want to hurry
along slowly.
Doris That's it!
Sissy Hurry along slowly, he used to say!
Doris That's it!
Sissy We're in no rush...
Doris That's it!
Sissy I mean we're not going anywhere fast, are we?
Doris Not today, we're not!
Sissy We're not going anywhere fast...

Jean notices a bus coming in the distance

Jean Is this them?
Sissy This is them...
Doris That's it, then!
Sissy This is us then, girls... Three days in Heidelberg. If I don't get a cuckoo
clock I'll eat my bloody hat...
Jean Is this us?
Sissy This is us, Jean, yeah...
Jean My bloody feet are all swelled up, look, and that's before we bloody
start.

Sissy Oh, she's on about her bloody feet, and we haven't even got on the coach yet!

Musical sting. The Lights open out. Sissy, Jean and Doris take off their headscarves and handbags. Larry, Stick and Frank re-appear

Stick It was their first time with Larards, and they were serious complainers; you could see it written all over them.
Larry Well, they were stuck over a wheel, that was the first problem... And the second problem was...
Frank We weren't Wallace Amold!
Larry We picked the Marx brothers up outside the Arndale Centre in Doncaster.

Musical sting. The Lights fade to focus in another area of the stage. Here we see Larry, Frank and Stick become Wally, Len and Brian. This is achieved by the three men wearing flat caps. They sit waiting for the bus. Frank plays Len. Larry plays Wally. Stick plays Brian

Wally Thing is though, Brian, it's your savings, isn't it, Len? It's what you've saved all your life for...
Len It is, ar!
Wally This is what I'm saying ... it's what you've planned for and look at it...
Brian It's all about money, Wally!
Wally Well, it is, ay! I mean look at me. I've nowt to come, have I? Nowt to live on! I mean since our lass, I've paid the house off, put a bit of sommat in the Halifax to stick me in a hole and a bit for run out like this ... and that's my lot!
Len Well ay...
Wally You can have worked all your life, but that doesn't mean blob any more. I'm telling thee we don't exist...
Brian Ay, there's a lot of us though, Wally...
Wally And this is what I'm saying, you see. It's about unification of a workforce, isn't it? There's a lot of uz in the same position but we've got no bloody power base, have we...
Len Bus is here...
Wally Have we?

The three men start to rise slowly. This is clearly a difficult and painful act for them since they have been seated for some time and have stiffened substantially

Brian Well no, that's right! Oh hell...

Len Oggghh!

Wally And that's another bloody thing, isn't it? Nobody ever tells you about all the sodding aches and pains you're going to get! I'm telling thee it's all a conspiracy.

Brian Well ay, tha might be right yet, Wally!

Wally It's a conspiracy tha sees, the working man gives his all and gets bugger all back!

Brian Ay, he's right.

Wally I mean twenty years ago would you have been happy going on a bus trip? Would you hell. We didn't save up for this, did we?

Brian Twenty years ago we'd go on the club trip...

Wally Ay, I know but what I'm saying is, we've got no security, have we ... it's all about money... Now if it was me, I wouldn't have interest rates low like that!

The Lights change. Larry, Stick and Frank take off their hats to reveal themselves once more

Stick We needed to watch those three, I said to Larry: "If we're not careful they might get to Germany and try to take over the rest of Europe". To say that they were all old mates they had a funny way of showing it!

Larry From Donny to Pontefract, one of my old haunts; to pick up two couples...

Frank Colin and May and their son Martin.

Stick Martin was forty-six, and never said owt, but at the pick-up his mother talked about him as if he'd got the wit of Michael Barrymore!

Frank (*putting on a hat*) I thought he was sweet!

Stick (*donning a bobble*) I didn't believe any of what she said, and his anorak didn't convince me!

The Lights change

May Oh, I know he looks quiet, but once he gets on the bus you'll be surprised. Won't they? Don't get him going, for goodness sake. Once you get him going there's no stopping him. Is there?

Martin No!

May He'll have you laughing like a drain. Won't you?

Martin Yeah!

May I mean he used to work at Ponte races course, didn't you?

Martin Yeah!

May And he'd come home with such stories, wouldn't you?

Martin Yeah!

May Have uz laughing for ages. Wouldn't you?

Martin Yeah.
May And eat? He can eat two pies more than a pig, can't you?
Martin I can, yeah!
May Forty-six ... and I still have to wash his hair sometimes, don't I?

May and Martin move US, *Larry picks up their cases and takes them* US

Larry Then we had Dot and Harry, both in their seventies! It was the first
time they'd been on a coach trip for years. It was the first time they'd been
anywhere for nine months! They were a Mack and Mabel all right; he never
gave her roses...

*As the Lights change, Stick and Frank become Dot and Harry. Harry wears
a baseball cap with "San Francisco" enscribed on it. Dot wears glasses and
moves extremely gingerly. They are in their seventies*

Dot I didn't really want to come, to be honest. I mean the last time we went
away it was two years ago to Fuengirola and I haven't been right since,
what with one thing and another. If it's not my heart, it's my stomach...
Harry Don't tell him all your ailments, Dot, we want to get there today...
Dot Have you rung our Janice?
Harry I've rung her, I've told her we're here...
Dot She put us up to this.
Larry Shall we get you on?
Dot I hope I'm not on a wheel, I can't bear it if I'm on a wheel. I was on a
wheel when I went to Blackpool fifteen years ago and I don't think I've got
over it, it affected my balance did that!
Larry You're at the front. But there's only one toilet so if you could stick
to wees only...
Dot Well, that's a relief because when he gets on you can't get him off!
Harry He doesn't want to know that...
Dot How do you know what he wants to know?
Harry I don't...
Dot How long will it be?
Larry Shorter than you think...
Dot Three buses? A lot more to pick up, then?
Larry Just sit back and enjoy the video. We'll have you there in no time.
Dot What is it?
Larry *The King and I.*
Dot *The King and I*? I could be in it! I've seen it that many times!
Larry Ay, good though, isn't it?
Dot "It's a puzzlement!"
Harry It bloody is living with you! Come on, let's get you on!

Dot We can't lift owt, we're both in a mess now! Never thought it would
come to this but...

The Lights change. Dot and Harry drift US, *to become Frank and Stick again,
as Larry picks up their cases and takes them* US, *securing them in the luggage
hold*

Larry Nearly there ... only another one and we're off...
Stick Coffee machine's broken on mine by the way; so we'll have to sort that
out...
Frank We coasted through Rotherham, picking up all the way.
Larry I've seen me picking up as far south as Leicester, and that was for a
shopping hop to Calais.
Frank In Sheffield we get the last two on ... after a struggle to find them.
Stick They reckon there's one born every minute. I think in this case there
were two born.

*During the following, Stick becomes Mollie and Frank becomes Connie, both
putting on smart hats*

Larry Molly and Connie were sisters... They thought they were a cut above
the others ... but we found out that their shop had gone bust and all they
owned is what they stood up in...

Mollie and Connie speak in refined Yorkshire accents

Connie I thought we had to wait by Jessops!
Larry At the bus station!
Mollie I said we should be here... Connie thought Jessops...
Connie I spoke to the lady in the office...
Mollie Jessops she thought.
Connie Well, I did ... only because she said so; so automatically I thought
that's where you'd want us to wait...
Mollie Which coach are we on...?
Larry You're with Stick... Third coach, at the back. He's a nice lad is Stick,
you'll be all right with him.
Connie Is there a coffee, I am absolutely parched.

*Stick and Frank become themselves once more. Larry places another couple
of cases under the luggage compartment*

Stick Thanks for them two! Mad as a biscuit both of them!
Larry Out on to the motorway then! Snake through Sheffield and head
south...

Frank First stop Leicester Forrest...
Stick We convoy down the M1 with three full coaches...
Frank All off 'em settling in nicely...
Larry On mine the Beverly Sisters started the singing off. You always know
it's going to be a good trip if the singing starts early!

*The Lights change. Larry, Stick and Frank are caught in a tighter light. They
begin to sing* On Mother Kelly's Doorstep *as the characters on Larry's bus.
They are having a good time*

  During the Light change, Frank exits

*We are at Leicester Forrest services. Larry lights up a cigarette, Stick stands
nearby*

Stick Last 'un, then?
Larry Ay, last 'un!
Stick Thought about what you're going to do?
Larry Thought me and our lass might go on a bus trip!
Stick Nice.
Larry Oh ay, only the best...
Stick Bit of a busman's holiday, isn't it?
Larry Don't know what I'm going to do, to be right. I've seen all the bloody
world already, nowhere left, is there. I might end up at Redcar, do a bit of
fishing.

A beat

Stick Where's this missing one got to then?
Larry Frank's gone to check the bogs!
Stick There's allus one missing from yours, isn't there? What do you do,
Larry, sing to 'em...?
Larry It wouldn't be Leicester Forrest if I didn't have one missing, would it?

Stick looks out at speeding traffic

Stick Have you seen the speed some of these silly sods travel at? Half of 'em
are on the bloody phone. Always rushing somewhere.

  Frank has become Sissy off stage, and enters

She's here, look... Just been to buy herself another ten thousand fags! Silly
old sod...

Larry You'll get there...

Stick I'll kill myself first...

Larry Come on, Sissy love, we're over here!

Sissy I got on the wrong bus...

Larry Trying to escape?

Sissy I got on the wrong bus... Went to the loo and got on the wrong bus.

Larry You'll tell me owt!

Sissy They never wait!

Larry Well, we have...

Sissy I thought Jean was still in there, you see. I thought sommat had happened, so I looked under the door, thought I could see her feet. Coz she said her feet were swelling up. I bent over, and had a look, but all the feet looked swelled up to me. I went bloody dizzy with bending over. Got up, didn't know where I was...

Larry You're all right now though!

Sissy I got on the Disneyland bus...

Larry Wishful thinking that was...

Sissy I'm bloody useless with directions...

Larry And I was going to ask you if you wanted to drive.

Sissy Me? I've never driven, never had the call for it!

Larry Ay well...

Sissy A lot of them in there...

Larry Is there...

Sissy Asian lot... Can't move for 'em in there...

Larry Where would the NHS be without 'em, love...

Sissy I got on the Disneyland bus, I must be going low, and they didn't wait, did they? Old people, you know, they're a bloody nuisance at times. And it was me who got the singing going; but they didn't wait for me, did they? I'll tell them about that when I get back on...

Sissy becomes Frank US

Stick If I ever get like that...

Larry She's smashing, mate...

Stick I'm glad she's on yours...

Larry Nearly there, Stick lad!

Stick We've only come a hundred miles...

Larry Nearly there.

Stick We pulled back out on to the motorway, and the singing bug must have spread through the lot of 'em. After about ten minutes, I had everybody on my bus singing!

They begin to sing "If You Were the Only Girl In the World"

Music. The Lights change. Stick slowly steps into a spotlight. The mood is changing

Stick Five miles north of Milton Keynes; the road cones start. We file into single file like school kids going to assembly. And there on the opposite side, framed like a film set, is a caravan and a car upturned!

Frank Everybody looks...

Stick Flipped over as a toy, brand new; just out of its box, bent and twisted by the bad boy of motorways.

Larry It's a reminder...

Stick We stream past slowly like mourners paying respect, two bodies bolt upright, but upside down; their faces bleached white, can be shocked no more! Him saved up everything for the caravan he wanted; her a little woman who wanted a place in the sun, and some Kendal mint cake.

Frank Killed outright as a tanker from Antwerp made light work of their Skoda.

Stick And behind me I have the Sisters of No Mercy who follow up their opening number with a medley of songs from the shows...

Larry I bloody love it...

Stick Folkestone is a long way south...

Larry Nearly there...

The Lights change. Stick, Frank and Larry begin to grab the cases from the luggage hold and stack them C

Frank We usually stop at the Starbeck Hotel. It says it's got good parking, cabaret and a sea view.

Larry Well, the parking is on the street...

Frank The cabarets are usually naff...

Stick And if you stand on the fire escape near the back you can just see the sea... It's three miles away but it's good enough for a bus trip...

Larry It's not a bad little place. It's a two star B 'n' B that thinks it's the Savoy. It's run by Sam and Sammy, who've both been club acts... We usually pile the cases outside, whilst Raymond and Clive...

Stick Who are both queers!

Larry Come and keep us up to date with the gossip...

Stick and Frank become Ray and Clive respectively. They take off their coats to indicate character change. Ray and Clive start to pick up the cases

Ray Right, let's get these shifted, we'll have them up in no time!

Clive You should've been here last night, talk about laugh. We had a party in from Scotland going down to Paris, dancing on the tables ... weren't they?

Ray Wicked. Up all night, some of 'em. Oh, don't mind me... What have they got in here? How long are you going for?

Larry I know, Phileas Fogg didn't take this much.

Ray Mind you, he went up in a balloon.

Clive Now stop it...

Ray I can't help it!

Clive What are they like then, this lot?

Larry Pensioners mostly...

Ray Ex-miners...?

Larry Ex-dockers...!

Ray Ay, thrown on the scrap heap like everybody else. I mean look at me, I worked for Metal Box in Keighley before I came down here, and they shut that!

Larry Ay, you've told me before.

Ray I mean if you can't work a computer or answer a phone at a call centre these days they just don't want you.

Clive Well, nobody wants you...

Ray Oh, shut up, you ... isn't he awful? It's Blair's Britain, isn't it?

Clive Oh, don't set him off on that...

Ray It's somebody's, it's not mine...

Clive He's raving commy him, you know! He's a raving sommat any way!

Ray Hey you!

Clive I'll have a screaming dickie fit if he keep going on about politics. Politics is people he says; ay and I've told him, it's not little people like us, not any more. We don't have a bloody say in it, do we? I mean I voted for William Hague anyway. So...

Larry Oh dear...

Clive Well, he had such a nice face, didn't he? That's what I go on!

Clive and Raymond lift the cases and move them off stage

Larry I don't judge. I never have. I think they're nice lads. They don't mess with me, because they know there's nowt in it for 'em! Stick can't bear 'em! He says we should stop somewhere where there's right folk. He says he can't see what him on the bottom gets out of it anyway ... if it was him, he says he'd want to be the one on top... He's a funny bloke is Stick. But I wouldn't want to be stranded on a desert island with him...

Music

As Sissy and Jean enter, Larry becomes Doris

Sissy We're not eating in the hotel, Doris...

Doris Aren't we?

Sissy I was just saying ... stuck on the wheel...

Doris I know.

Jean You should have said sommat!

Sissy I don't like...

Doris No...

Sissy ...you know, causing any bother... I don't like... But I mean when you've paid for it, you don't expect...

Jean Hey them two in front of us ... from Pontefract...

Doris I think he's a bit slow...

Jean And three men on their own...

Sissy Wife's died...

Jean I heard him say...

Sissy Oh dear...

Doris Are we going back for tea?

Sissy Well, I'm not...

Doris No, I'm not...

Sissy I mean I never do anyway, I've put some sandwiches up for us. I mean you can please yourself, but you never know what you're eating when you're out, that's what I think! I always wrap my own up. Cheese and ham, cheese and tomato or just cheese, I mean you can't go wrong with a cheese spread, can you?

Doris Well ay!

Jean I don't eat much when I'm abroad anyway.

Sissy I've done about fifty-seven.

Doris They're quiet, aren't they? Them at the front! She looks nervous...

Sissy First time away...

Jean I don't think she's well.

Doris She's not well!

Jean I didn't think she was.

Sissy They both look badly to me!

Jean Mind you, I feel a bit...

Sissy Are your feet swelling up again?

Jean It's not my feet so much... I keep having these spinning dos...

Sissy Oh, I've had them, have a cheese sandwich, you'll be all right with that!

Jean No, I think it's the cheese that makes me spin.

Sissy Do you know, I can eat pounds of cheese and it does nowt to me!

Doris Hey, I was thinking there's three blokes on their own and three of us, we might get lucky...

Sissy Ay and we would be and all, they're all sharing the same bedroom.

Music. The Lights change. Sissy, Doris and Jean become Wally, Len and Brian. The Lights indicate we are now in the men's bedroom. Wally looks out at the fourth wall, a window gobo picks him out

Wally Can't see the sea...

Brian It's a good job you didn't bring the cat, Wally...

Wally I couldn't swing it in here...

Len Not a bad ride down really. My legs have all swollen up but...

Wally They advertise this as a sea view, you know. You could take 'em to the Trades Description for that.

Len I'm still travelling.

Wally I mean I'm not a prude, but three in a room. Has there been a mix up?

Brian Ay, I mean what if we get lucky?

Wally Last time I got lucky, Brian, it was thirty years ago, I don't want another one...

Brian Neither do I!

Wally I wouldn't want to go through all that again.

Brian Nor me.

Len Some good things about it though, Wally.

Wally Well ay, there is.

Len Some good things about it though!

Wally They don't last very long though, do they, Len?

Len Depends how you do it, does it, Brian?

Brian Ay, it does, ay... Mind you, I can't do a lot for our lass now my knees have given up on me!

Wally Well, you can please yourself but...

Brian No, our lass is all right ... but I've just learnt to accept less as I've got older.

Wally Well, I wouldn't have built this hotel like this, I mean there's no parking space, garden or owt!

A beat

Brian Oh hell, Len?

Len What?

Wally Oh... I've just got it.

Brian Has tha parted with the wind?

Len What?

Wally Have you let one go?

Len Course I have; you don't think I always smell like this, do you?

Wally It's going to be a long night, Len, if you keep doing that, sunshine!

Music. As the Lights change, Len exits

Wally and Brian become Stick and Larry again and move DS. They are caught in gobos as they look out towards the sea

Stick It's out there somewhere...

Larry What is?

Stick The sea...

Larry I still can't quite believe we go under it! Bloody amazing...

Stick We might come back with more than we expected if we're not careful
... fighting to get in now, aren't they? You don't want some little friends
under your bus, Larry, do you, what would Dennis say about that?

Larry He'd not be happy, would he?

A beat

Stick Are you going to watch t' turn?

Larry Not again, I've seen it six times.

Stick Might have changed.

Larry Well, it's not changed in the last six years.

Stick You should get up...

Larry You'd be surprised...

Stick That's what everybody says...

Larry No... I'll leave it to the professionals... I don't want to frighten
anybody.

Stick Well, aren't you going in for t' Bingo?

Larry No, I'll stand out here, why change a winning formula? I've been
standing here on this run for six years!

Stick Well, it's fairly simple is Bingo tha knows?

Larry I know it is, but I never bloody win owt!

Music. The Lights change

> *The central doorway opens, smoke appears and Dolly, a woman singer/
> comedian enters. She walks* DS *into a spotlight* C *and sings a verse and
> chorus of "Pal of My Cradle Days"*

Dolly Are we all right, then? Are we all right? And we're all from Yorkshire,
are we? God's country, isn't it? I came down here fifteen years ago, I
thought the streets were paved with Steradent. No, I did, honest! They are!
They don't bury people in Folkestone, you know! No, they stand 'em up
in bus shelters! No, I'm serious. Are you from Scargill country? Or posh
Yorkshire, Richard Whiteley country? You know how they define it,
Yorkshire humour, don't you? There's a comic on at a club and two blokes
are stood at the bar and one says to the other what do you think to the comic?
And the other one says; he's all right, if you like laughing.

Larry They usually leave me a piece of Bakewell tart and I have that later...

Dolly So you're going down the Rhine, lucky sods! No, I think you are! It's
lovely down there. And you're going to see *The Student Prince*. What is

it? "Come, boys, let's all be gay boys". It's popular in here! No, it is. No,
I'm only joking. Drink, drink, drink. It's all that, isn't it? Lift your stein and
drink your beer, well, that's all he's been doing all night, so you should be
all right then.

Stick I can't stomach Bakewell tart...

Larry Oh ay...

Stick Reminds me of old age...

Larry I like it...

Dolly No, you all look lovely, no, you do! Did you hear this one! She gets
up one morning and she says to her husband "What am I wearing that's
new?" And he's just reading the paper or playing with a glass, like you are
... and he say "I don't know, are you wearing a new blouse?" And she says
"No", and he says "You've had your hair done?" And she says "No" and
he says "I don't know, what are you wearing that's new?" And she says...

All I'm wearing a gas mask!

Larry Same old routine...

Stick Not a bad response tonight. You usually get a few "I've heard its"!

Larry Ay, usually from thee!

Stick It's about all they want though, isn't it? Jokes they've heard before.

Larry Let them eat cake, eh?

Stick Let 'em eat Bakewell tart!

Dolly So she says to the doctor "I can't reach an orgasm unless my husband
does something kinky". So the doctor says "In that case I'd better send you
to see a specialist".

Larry This sounds like a new 'un...

Stick Shh, listen...

Dolly So she goes to see the specialist...

Stick I don't think Mack and Mabel are keen on this one...

Larry Seven Brides is all ears, look at him...

Dolly And the specialist says "Right, take off all your clothes, lay on my
couch, I'm going to turn off the light and in the next twenty minutes, I'm
going to do something very kinky...

Larry We might need an ambulance here...

Stick Ssshh!

Dolly So she eagerly gets on the couch ... look at him, look at this one here
... he's living it, aren't you. You're there, darling, aren't you? ... anyway!
So she gets on the couch, the light goes off. And twenty minutes later the
light goes on. He hasn't touched her. And she says to him "I thought you
were going to do something kinky"? He says "I have done, I've had a shit
in your handbag"...

Stick That's a new 'un...

Dolly Listen, you've been a lovely audience, but I just wanted to tell you this,
last week ... and this is true ... last week I was on here and after I'd done

my set I went to the bar, and somebody bought me a drink; you'll not know anything about that what with you coming from Yorkshire ... but I went to the bar and somebody bought me a drink and he says to me "Do you know, that was fantastic, you're the best drag act I've ever seen". I says "Drag act? I'm a bloody woman, you cheeky bastard!" Now that might not be funny but it is the truth... Thank you for listening to me... And have a great holiday, won't you...

Music. The Lights change

Dolly disappears in a cloud of smoke

Stick and Larry drift DC

Larry At five o'clock the next morning I got a knock on my door. One of the Beverley sisters had taken badly.
Stick Raymond was on night duty and all.
Larry Well, I didn't relish the thought of being downstairs on my own with him, but you do what you've got to in the circumstances. He'd done what he could for her ... but she didn't look well.
Stick They thought at first it was food poisoning but she hadn't eaten in the hotel, so that was ruled out...
Larry She reckoned it was some cheese sandwich that she'd had! Anyway, we sent for a locum, and he didn't turn up till ten to six the next morning...
Stick I told thee, didn't I, they're a liability that lot!

The Lights change. Larry and Stick are sorting out the cases, and baggage

Larry Looks like it's going to be a scorcher!
Stick It'll probably rain in Germany, knowing my luck! Be just what I want, sat inside for a week playing bloody snap with the Marx brothers...
Larry I never want to be a member of a club that would have me as a member, Stick.
Stick You what?

Frank enters carrying some cases

Frank Doctor's still with her.
Larry Well, we can't wait for her much longer! If we miss the Chunnel connection, job's a bad 'un.
Stick We'll just have to leave her if she's off it!
Larry I don't want to be late on my last run, it doesn't seem fair to the others.
Stick What's Doctor say...?

Frank I don't know… She's Nigerian or sommat, I can't make it out. She speaks like a little mouse…

Larry Let me go and have a word with her…

Stick Ay, he speaks mouse does Larry… It's Mickey Mouse most of the time like…

Larry They're looking for comics in here, Stick, if you fancy it. Raymond told me he'd got his eye on you!

Stick We're snookered if we miss that crossing… We'll not be nearly there then, Larry… We'll be nearly, not there!

Larry exits

Frank helps Stick sort the cases

Frank She doesn't look well, to be honest!

Stick This is what I was saying last night, we've got all these asylum seekers coming here, and what do they get when they get here? I mean it's not as if everything's bloody perfect, is it?

Frank All her ankles are swelled up! She says she's got chest pains!

Stick I mean my mother waited two years for a hip operation, and now they reckon the wait's going to be longer because they can't get donors…

Frank You don't need a donor for an hip operation, you soft pillock…

Stick I'm just saying everything's not as it should be here! I mean look at the bloke in Hemsworth; had a heart attack and they couldn't get to him, he ended up dying in the bloody fire engine, poor sod! I mean if these asylum seekers knew how bad it was here…

Frank Well, it just might be worse where they are, you dollop…

Larry enters. He lights a cigarette

The remainder of the cases are packed. The conversation is barbed but friendly

Larry Jean's daughter's going to come for her. They're going to let her stop in that room until she gets here.

Stick So the damp should kill her if nowt else.

Larry Sissy's heart-broken, but she's not going back, she says she's going down the Rhine no matter what. You'd think she was on a promise.

Frank Maybe she is.

Stick What about that woman from Hull who met that GI she'd known in the War! Must have been seventy-nine, and she never went home to her husband. And that is Gospel.

Larry Course she did!

Stick She never did!

Larry She was on my bus.

Stick Larry, she never came back!

Larry She did, I bloody know her... I've seen her in the supermarket! I've spoke to her, I've seen her with her husband. They used to own a bike shop down Princess Avenue.

Stick He's been on this run too long he has, he's losing the plot!

Larry Tha'll end up like me, don't worry about it... You'll all end up like me.

Stick I bloody hope not!

Larry I dream bloody motorways... Miles and miles of bloody tarmac. I waken up and I've no idea where I am!

Stick I thought you couldn't sleep?

Larry That's obviously when I do sleep, you contrary chuff!

Frank (*to Stick*) He's got a bear on because he wanted Johnny Mac's run, didn't you?

Larry I bet he did and all...

Stick Why does he get all the good runs, anyway? Look at him this week; Tossa de Mar!

Larry Ay, all tossers go there!

Stick He's got a coach full of sixth formers from Pocklington. Girls most of 'em, on some language course. I spoke to him last night; he said they were nearly all half naked by the time they got to Newark!

Frank He'll be tossing hissen crackers then!

Larry He wouldn't be able to keep his eyes on the bloody road, him, if he went.

Stick Well, it beats this bollocks. It'll be just my luck to get stranded in the bloody Chunnel!

Larry (*to the audience*) And we did, we were stuck right smack in the middle of the sodding thing for two hours. The Marx brothers just stood staring out of the window looking into all that blackness. Well, I supposed they were used to it!

They become Wally, Len and Brian, peering into the fourth wall

Len Not much of a view this time, Wally...

Wally And still no sea view...

Brian It's up above us somewhere...

Wally Bloody black out there...

Len I think some of the women thought they'd be able to see fish.

Wally Black out there...

Len One old lass said "Would the water come in?" I told her if it was going to come in it would have come in thousands of years ago...

Brian That's right!

Wally Like Melton field at Wath, can tha remember?

Brian More height here though.

Len There was nine ton of water for every ton of coal we got out!

Wally Must have taken a bloody cutter to cut an hole like this! I don't think I would have cut it out like that...

Brian How would you have cut it out then, Wally...?

Wally Well, it doesn't look right, looks like we're too close to the side.

Len Funny, isn't it? We spent all our lives in a bloody hole in the ground and now they're charging us to go through one!

Brian They never charged you to go down Wath, did they, Len?

Len Scargill was right, you know... There's thousands of tons down here... And we're importing bloody coal from Poland.

Wally Well, I'll tell you this; I wouldn't have designed this tunnel like this, it's a mess. It all wants knocking down and re-doing if you ask me!

Brian Ay well, let's get out of it first, Wally, before you start doing that, shall we...?

Len How long have we been now?

Brian A good hour...

Len Ay... They never advertised this in the brochure, did they? Being stuck under the tunnel for a bloody hour...

Brian They might be doing it just for us, Len, keeping us down here in the dark because we're ex-miners.

Len Ay, that's right, they might think we like it!

Wally Well, I would never have cut this tunnel out like that!

Len Hey, what if we get trapped here?

Brian Shall we sing?

Wally Do you think they'll hear us?

They start singing: fade into the drivers

All   Answer me oh my love,
                  Tell me just what sin have I been guilty of...
                  Tell me how I came to lose your love...
                  Please answer me, sweetheart...

                  You were mine yesterday
                  Now it seems your love has gone away...
                  Do dee do dee do dee do dee dey
                  Please answer me sweetheart...

Stick Four more hours of mindless babbling led by the Sisters of Murder from Sheffield and we've sung every song in the repertoire. We arrived in Boppard about two-ish!

The Lights change. Frank, Stick and Larry take up the story

Frank We were booked in a hotel overlooking the river.
Larry Beautiful, everywhere there's hanging baskets! And the Rhine, as
  busy as a motorway … it's a proper river, do you know what I mean, like
  a river should be…
Frank The hotel's friendly enough, everybody speaks English. The stairs are
  a problem for some of ours; and the lifts won't behave.

Frank and Larry become Sissy and Doris

Stick There's cuckoo clocks to buy if you need one, and there's some
  German plonk; that Riesling; I mean it's like piss to me, but everybody
  ends up getting a bottle like it's some sort of national duty. Along the
  promenade German youths hang about wearing T-shirts and two ton of
  face studs. They pose and watched our lot get off. Some of the kids have
  got blue hair and red lips. Some of them have got red hair and blue lips. As
  they watched our lot spew out of the coach, I said to Frank: "I don't know
  who looks the most frightening."

The Lights change. Sissy and Doris make their way DS. *They are both ever so
stiff*

Sissy Bloody hell… Stiff…
Doris Oh ay…
Sissy That bloody wheel. I've got one leg longer than the other now.
Doris You've what?
Sissy I've got one leg longer than the other now!
Doris You'll be walking round in circles if you're not careful.
Sissy I'm like that anyway with this hip!
Doris I need to get some tea…
Sissy Well, I've got a sandwich left if…
Doris I think I need something warm…
Sissy They do sausage…
Doris I'm not supposed to eat sausage.
Sissy They do sausage…
Doris I'm not supposed to touch it!
Sissy They have a lot of sausage.
Doris I'm not supposed to touch sausage, but now and again I like a little bit.
  Kenny Knowles did the best sausage I've ever had.
Sissy I fancy a bit of sausage myself to be honest…

Stick picks up a number of cases and takes them off stage

Stick Room 216. Better watch the lift, they reckon it's got a mind of its own.

Sissy We'll have to find out about Jean!

Doris Can somebody ring up?

Sissy She wasn't well, wasn't Jean!

Doris She wasn't!

Sissy I told her "you're not well; don't come", but she...

Doris Wouldn't listen...

Sissy Just wouldn't...

Doris Couldn't tell her...

Sissy She just didn't want to know... And now look where she is...

Doris Where is she?

Sissy Well, we don't know, do we, but she's not here, is she?

Doris No, she's not, no... Where is she?

Sissy She's in Folkestone, isn't she!

Doris And her daughter having to drive all that way to pick her up...?

Sissy Ay, I know, and she's a chiropodist!

Doris It makes you wonder, doesn't it?

Sissy It does... It makes you wonder what's it all coming to.

A beat

Doris I do right fancy a bit of sausage, to be honest.

As Doris and Sissy exit, Stick enters and picks up a few more cases

Stick Most people like to get a feel for their rooms when we get here. Seven Brides decided to go on a river cruise to see the Loreli... Three hours later they'd come back and May, his mother, had lost her teeth over the side of the boat. Apparently Martin didn't like her looking over the side ... so he'd held on to her so tight that her bottom set fell out as a barge passed them on its way up to Hamburg. Martin had a cheeky smile on his face when I told him that Interpol would be hunting for the rest of the body for the next ten years!

Frank and Larry enter and pick up cases

Frank There's usually three or four complaints every hour... But the hotel are quite good with 'em really, and it's all the usual stuff...

Stick It's too hot in our room!

Larry It's too cold in ours!

Stick I can't close the window!

Frank I can't open one...!

Stick There's no English telly!

Larry The best I heard was from a woman from Harrogate who told the receptionist that she didn't like the room, the carpet was a mess, the toilet smelt, there was no lock on the door and the wallpaper didn't match the curtains...

Frank Ay, she got a complimentary crème de menthe and that was the end of it!

Music. The Lights change. Stick, Frank and Larry become Wally, Len and Brian. They are c, the cases make a small room for them to act in. Gobos pick out their room

Brian That's a river, Wally...

Wally That is a river.

Len Ay, that is a river.

Wally Ay, it's a working river is that...

Brian They know how to make things work out here, don't they.

Wally Oh ay...

Brian Well, it was all re-built, wasn't it?

Wally River wasn't...

Brian No, the river wasn't...

Len They all seem to be able to do things better than us, don't they? We just close things down!

Wally They've unemployment now though, tha knows...

Brian Serves 'em right!

Len I mean look at the Americans, they can do stuff a lot better than uz. I mean did tha see when they landed that shuttle? Just brought it down like an aeroplane. I watched that for six hours.

Wally I watched that an all!

Len Wasn't it amazing?

Wally Well, it was but I'll tell you sommat... I would never had landed it like that!

Len What?

Wally I would never have landed that shuttle like that...

Brian Bloody hell, Wally, they spent twenty years working it out.

Wally I'm not bothered, I would never have landed it like that...

Len Hell fire, Wally ... how did your lass ever live with thee?

Wally How do you mean?

Len I bet she couldn't do anything right! Their lass is in labour, poor sod, their Tony pops out, and midwife says "Mr Wall, it's a boy" ... and all Wally says to their lass is "Well, I wouldn't have done it like that...!"

Piano music. The Lights change. Len, Brian and Wally become Stick, Frank and Larry, take up the story, and enjoy a sandwich

Larry Down in the dining-room a pianist trotted through some Chopin ... we don't know if he's good, bad or making it up as he bloody goes along, but it feels cultured...

Stick It's a load of wank really because our lot get separated into a room at the back of the hotel. If they didn't feel like second class citizens when they arrived, they did then! Mind you, like I say, they're too thick to know any different...

Larry And over tea I heard the same old conversations.

Frank Miners worked harder than fishermen...

Stick Three years on a waiting list...

Frank Well, we didn't vote...

Stick What's Labour party done for uz...

Frank Well, our Sandra's a teacher...

Stick Well, our Janet's a nurse...

Frank Well, our Kenny won the lottery...

Larry Well, the politicians have just given themselves another bloody pay rise, haven't they?

Stick It's one rule for one, and one for another!

Frank Saved up all my life and look at the interest rates...

Stick I've nowt to live on, me ... and they've given themselves a better pension deal...

Frank And somewhere in the middle of all that, as we shared some of Sissy's cheese and tomato sandwiches, you can just about hear Wally tell the pianist...

Stick I wouldn't have played it like that!

Music. The Lights change. Frank becomes Sissy. Stick stands US *with a beer and listens to a radio. We hear the music from the radio. Larry lights a cigarette. Gobos tell us it is a balmy September evening*

Larry I don't think I'd ever seen t' Rhine looking so calm! Suddenly I was looking at trees and filling up. I've even taken an interest in animal welfare. Hell fire, when we had a dog I used to kick it from arse hole to breakfast time!

Sissy enters. She is smoking

Sissy Lovely night ... cooled off a bit?

Larry Ay, it is!

Sissy It's a *Summertime in Heidelberg* night!

Larry Ay, it is, ay... Are you going to see it?

Sissy Oh ay... I'm a fan.

Larry Mario?

Sissy Oh ay...

Larry Me and all! I love owt he's done. I prefer his modern stuff ahead of his classical but... *Student Prince, The Desert Song*, owt like that...

Sissy My feet swell up in the heat but...

Larry Better now it's cooled off, then...

Sissy I was just talking to her from Pontefract. Her nerves are all over the shop. Not been away from home for years ... can't relax, thinks she's going to be badly again.

Larry Oh dear...

Sissy She says she's promised herself a visit to Heidelberg! Hope to God she makes it! I don't think Jean taking bad helped her nerves much.

Larry No.

Sissy Mind you I told her, when he's ready for you he'll come and get you!

Larry Ay well...

Sissy You're a long time dead, aren't you?

Larry Ay, you are!

Sissy I've done bloody everything me, I've smoked all my life, drank myself bloody badly, eaten what I want; ... and I've allus thought the same.

Larry Have you?

Sissy You'll know when your time's up!

Larry Do you think so?

Sissy Oh ay!

Larry Ay well, you've to take it while it's there, then?

A beat

Sissy Have you heard owt else about what's going off with Jean?

Larry Ay, I have, ay.

Sissy Oh ay?

Larry Ay ... it's er...

Silence

Sissy Oh dear!

Larry Ay!

Sissy Oh dear!

Larry I was going to tell you in the morning! Her daughter phoned the office.

Sissy Oh dear!

Larry Oh dear!

A beat

Sissy She'll not want them sandwiches, then?

Larry I wouldn't have thought so...

A beat

Sissy She knew she wasn't well... She told me in them toilets at Leicester Forrest. I thought she was constipated at first, but she said "Sissy, he's coming for me... I'm not going to get there, Sissy, he's coming for me, it's time for me to go". I told her not to be so daft... But I knew she was right...

Larry Oh dear...

Sissy All them bloody sandwiches and all...

Larry That's right...

Sissy Isn't it funny ... she knew he was coming for her... She knew he was coming for her...

Sissy walks US *and off*

Stick comes DS *and stands near to Larry*

Larry They don't pay you for that stuff, do they?

Stick I would have told her if tha'd wanted, tha knows!

Larry Well, she was on my coach, wasn't she?

Stick It happens, doesn't it?

Larry Ay, but I could have done without it on this trip though! You never know what's round the corner, do you?

Stick I shouldn't worry about that old lass. I mean half of these are on their way out anyway, aren't they?

Larry Well, I hope not! I hope I get back with at least something resembling the complement of what I set off with.

Stick Well, tha's already lost one...

Larry Ay, I don't want to lose any bloody more, do I?

A beat

Stick Where's Frank gone, then?

Larry She goes down to that bar at the end...

Stick I might pop down and have a drink with her!

Larry And that's another bloody thing, isn't it?

Stick What?

Larry Frankie!

Stick Tha still fancies her, does tha?

Larry She drives me crazy at times.

Stick Well, there tha goes then...

Larry How long has she been with us now, and nobody's cracked it with her, have they?

Stick Well, I thought she was a les for two years, so I kept my distance like!

Larry More of a challenge though!

Stick Johnny Mac reckons she's got a bloke in Hull prison. He's bloody crackers according to form! Why, are you thinking about giving it a go?

Larry I've got our lass though, haven't I?

Stick Go on, man, get stuck in! What has tha got to lose?

Larry I wouldn't mind, to be honest...

Stick Hey, everybody's in bed. Get down that bar, Larry, and start crooning to her, now that is an order! Come on here! You reckon to be a romantic, get down there and sing her sommat!

Larry No, not tonight...

Stick I'm telling thee, tha's gunna get lucky on this trip! Thee believe me! When we get to Heidelberg, do sommat romantic with her, take her to see the show, take her for a meal and then try and knob her one!

Larry Well, I don't think *The Student Prince* is the right show to take her to, to be honest!

Stick Why's that then?

Larry Well, I'm usually crying my eyes out by the end of it!

Stick Why's that?

Larry Well, he can't marry his true love, can he, because he's a bloody prince and she's the inn keeper's niece and his father dies so he has to go back to be the king, you soft bastard!

Stick I'm only asking.

Larry There's a section when Mario's voice comes in on the film, and oh bloody hell... I melt...

Stick Well, maybe Frank'd melt and all? You just have a think about that? (*He begins to move off*)

Larry Where's tha going?

Stick I'm going to that bar, have a drink with Frank; I can't sleep en-route anyway...

Stick exits

A spotlight slowly develops on Larry

Larry He was right, nobody sleeps en-route, I don't know if it's a strange bed or what? I stood outside watching the river. Inside I could see 'em all looking out of their bedroom windows... People afraid of the dark. They were still up; Mack and Mabel. He'd been down for some hot milk for her twice ... she was sat there looking through the window...

Music. The Lights change

We see Frank as Dot and Stick as Harry. Dot is looking out of the window.

Harry is dressed in pyjamas sited too high up the chest, and holding a glass of hot milk

Dot Can't get a signal on that phone... Must be the hills!

Harry Go to sleep!

Dot I can't...

Harry You'll be badly...

Dot We're such a long way from home though, aren't we? I mean how do they get an ambulance down here?

Harry You won't need an ambulance.

Dot I feel all shakey.

Harry Just try and go to sleep!

Dot I don't want to be badly again.

Harry You will be, if you don't get some sleep!

Dot My chest's all tight again.

Harry It's not...

Dot All these boats, look...

Harry What's keeping you awake, the boats, or your chest?

Dot Have we done the right thing?

Harry Just try and go to sleep...!

Dot I don't know if I'll make it back...

Harry You're fixed now, aren't you? Nothing to worry about. It's me who's in bloody danger, all this travelling, all this stress.

Dot Oh, don't you bloody start...

Harry You think you've got the monopoly on being badly...

Dot All this way from home, what if sommat goes wrong?

Harry Give it a miss, love...

Dot What are we doing here? In the middle of bloody nowhere?

The Lights change. Larry is caught in a spotlight, as the Light on Dot and Harry fades

Larry We call Boppard the "halfway house", but in truth we're three quarters of the way there. I think the news about Jean had got round, and that cast a cloud over everybody. They reckon that life's a journey, don't they, and it's the way you travel it... I started to think about Johnny Mac in Spain. Stick had told me that them kids were bonking each other senseless, and even though Johnny hadn't got a look in, at least he was surrounded by it... Next morning we're up and off early; we had to call at Rudeshiem for some wine-tasting before travelling down to Heidelberg...

Music: The Riff Song *from* The Desert Song

I still felt a bit maudlin about Jean that morning, to be honest. So to shake it off I played Mario singing "The Riff Song" from *The Desert Song* at full blast on my coach... You must have been able to hear it all down the bloody Rhine valley. Bugger 'em, I thought: that'll get 'em going... In fifty minutes we'd be tasting wine in Rudeshiem, and it felt absolutely natural for the Red Shadow to be back on the road...

Music swells. The Lights start a long fade

Larry begins to get the suitcases sorted as Frank and Stick enter with further suitcases

The marching rhythms of the music create a kind of routine as the coach drivers dump all the luggage back on the stage. Ready for the next part of their journey

The Lights fade to black. "The Riff Song" plays out

CURTAIN

ACT II

Music

Frank, Larry and Stick enter

They sit on a number of suitcases. They are clearly waiting for people to come back to the coaches

The Lights change

Stick How long do you think they're going to be now?

Frank Well, they're nearly all back, aren't they?

Larry My lot aren't.

Stick He doesn't train 'em right, that's why. I tell 'em a definite departure time, three or four times before they get off. And I tell 'em if they're not back by that time, I'll charge 'em a penalty fee or leave 'em for dead.

Frank I bet he does and all!

Stick I do!

Larry Fifteen minutes' grace isn't going to hurt though, is it?

Stick I don't know what they find to do, to be honest.

Larry They just saunter about, don't they?

Stick There's only about twenty shops in the whole town. I mean you see them staring in the windows of those bloody toy shops like they've lost the plot.

Frank Oh, he's off!

Larry Ay, I thought we'd done well!

Stick Well, you do...

Frank "They should shoot 'em"...

Stick Well, have you seen 'em? The women are salivating because they can legitimately go shopping, because there's sod all else to do and the men follow 'em about like mindless dummies! Just stood there... "Ummmm! Oh yes, love, that's lovely is that, love, let's buy one of them useless German knick-knacks that we'll never use for our Clarence: he'll love that!" "Oh yes, love, look at them, can you believe it, a jar of German pickled onions, we'll have two of them, mine herr! Danke!"

Larry He's such a sour sod!

Stick You'd see 'em and all, if you had a mind to look! They stand in their British Home Stores slacks, looking like they've lost the will to live.

Larry That's marriage for you that is. Don't you recognize it?

Frank Oh, don't!

Stick I mean come on, what would you rather be doing, watching some sixteen-year-olds go topless in Tossa de Mar, rubbing Ambre Solaire all over 'em, or stood with your lass looking at some decorated beer jugs?

Larry Well, ar but...

Stick Be honest with yourself, man, hell fire!

Larry Well, ah but...

Stick Well, ah but? What does that mean?

Larry Well, ah, I know but...

Stick What about you, Frank?

Frank Well, topless women don't do a lot for me!

Stick I was on about the men?

Frank Mind you, you know sometimes, you wonder what you might have missed in life!

Stick Exactly, and that's my point...!

Frank Well, it's what you do though, isn't it?

Stick Wonder what you might have missed? Exactly, we're always at the crossroads, mate!

Frank I can remember when we used to go to Cleethorpes as a kid. We always seemed to do the same thing, year in, year out! We'd walk to the sea front, play on the sands, have fish and chips, a game of bingo, play on the crazy golf, then go back on the sands. Then we'd have a bath, and walk about in the cold again before we went to bed. Then the next day it would be the same. It was the highlight of the holiday if my mam decided she would buy me and our Tina some new flip flops! Bloody hell ... when you think!

Larry It was Blackpool for us! If I had a pound for every time I'd done the Blackpool run...

Frank We thought Cleethorpes was a seaside resort and all. Then we moved to Hull and I realized I'd been having all my holidays on the mouth of a bloody river!

Stick I honestly don't know what these come for. In fact, I don't know why we run these trips at all! They seem utterly pointless.

Frank And when we started going to Palma, we got into a routine there and all. We'd get up, have a coffee at the same bar, buy an English paper from the same shop. Then we'd sit on the sands in the same place! Come off for siesta, go for a swim at the same time, have a shag more or less at the same time, and depending on how much Les had had to drink ... and if he'd got sunstroke...

Stick We're pedalling dreams but the reality is naff!

Larry What's new...?

Stick Well, the chance of some excitement is what keeps us going, Larry, surely. I'm not like you. I don't want to keep watching the sun set. That only tells me one thing that does ... time's going...

Frank It is today and that's for sure!

Larry Unless he's getting laid there's no point to anything!

Stick It's not even getting laid, it's the possibility that you might. That's what interests me, it's more or less the same with whoever...

Frank Oh, listen to him ... you're not doing it right, Stick!

Stick Well, it is for me...

Frank You should have been with some of the men I've been with...

Stick No, thanks...

Frank You'd change your bloody tune then. There's a lot of difference between ballet dancing and clog dancing, I can tell you, but they're both forms of dancing!

Larry It's a different culture when you're abroad though, isn't it? That's part of the attraction!

Stick Is it hell! If you go up to the top, where the cable car is, to that Christmas shop, you'll see 'em fighting to get in, just to buy a bauble for the Christmas tree! Yet you can get the self same baubles, for the same price, in that Yorkshire Garden Centre at Gilberdyke!

Frank Ay, he's got a point there actually coz we got some baubles from Giberdyke last year, and they were just the same!

A beat

Larry Aren't we all right?

Stick Well, this is crackers this is, it's like waiting to be bloody shot!

Larry speaks to the audience. Thereafter Stick and Frank do the same

Larry It took us two hours to get from Boppard to Rudeshiem. It should have taken us fifty minutes but we had to stop three times because fat Joyce from Greaseborough couldn't fit in the loo on my coach...

Frank ...And the veal she'd had didn't agree with her...

Stick It was the same old routine. Park up at the bottom by the station, usher 'em across the railway line and the road to see the church, the beer gardens, some knick-knack shops and get some more Euros. That alone takes 'em three hours!

Frank There's one of them little trains that takes you round the town and all...

Larry I saw Sissy and Doris going round on that eating their sandwiches.

Stick Martin and his mam and dad stayed down by the coach and had another picnic...

Frank They fascinated Stick...

Stick They did, they just sat and talked about gravel for two hours... And though she said he was funny, he didn't make her laugh once!

Larry There's a monument right up on the hillside, if you take the cable car you can see all down the Rhine Valley; it's right view, it takes about forty minutes to get up and you hang low in the cable car over some massive grape fields...

Frank The Marx brothers had gone up in one together... You could see 'em in the distance coming down...

Music. The Lights change. Frank, Stick and Larry become Wally, Len and Brian. They are seated together, and are holding on tight as their cable car bumps its way back down the hillside

Len Never liked heights...

Brian No...

Len Never did.

Brian We're not that high though, are we, Len?

Len Our young 'un allus wanted to go up the tower at Blackpool and I never would.

Brian I went up but ... never again...

Len Our lass took him up. I was stood there at the bottom. Frightened to death in case they didn't come back down. I felt like a bloody fraud after that.

Brian Ay you do, don't you! Kids!

Len Oh ay!

Brian They think you're some kind of superman ... and then they realize. I mean I told our Keith I'd played football for England; we were in a boarding house in Blackpool once, and he went and told all the tables at tea time...

Len That's kids for you, Brian...

Brian I didn't mind it so much except the bloke who ran the hotel used to manage Preston North End. He looked at me like I was half soaked or sommat!

Len Bloody kids!

Brian Oh ay...

A beat

Len Tha's quiet, Wally.

Wally Well, I'm saying nowt.

Brian He's got a huff on!

Len Why, what's up with thee?

Wally Well, it's like being out with our lass. Every time I open my mouth I'm bloody wrong, so I've decided not to say owt!

Brian Told you he'd got a huff on!
Len I can't believe tha'll be like for the rest of the trip though, Wally?
Wally Ay well, we'll see.

A beat

Len It's nice to have a bit of quiet though, isn't it, Brian?
Brian Well ay, it is, ay! He's been that quiet I thought he'd fallen off...
Wally I hadn't fallen off!
Len Oh, he's talking now, look!
Wally I was just thinking, that's all...
Len Oh, right then...
Brian That's bloody dangerous, isn't it?
Len Ay, tha doesn't want to be thinking at thy age, Wally.
Brian End up in t' bloody nuthouse...
Len What have you been thinking about?
Wally Well, when we were going up, I wondered why they hung these cable cars so low over the field.
Len Tha wouldn't have hung it like that, would tha?
Wally Well, I bloody wouldn't, no!
Brian He's off again, look...
Wally Well, you asked me...
Brian He's off again.
Wally Well, you bad pigs...
Len Off again...
Wally Right, that's it, this time. I shalln't open my mouth a-bloody-gain!
Len I don't believe in miracles, does tha, Brian?
Brian No, I don't, no!
Wally You're bad pigs the both of you.
Brian Come on, Wally, we're only pulling your leg, aren't we, Len?
Len Oh ay, I wouldn't have reacted like that, would tha, Brian?

The Lights change. Music. Brian, Len and Wally become Frank, Stick and Larry once more

Larry Back down by the coaches we were still waiting for the last two to show up. Typical and all, wasn't it? They had to be on my bloody coach.
Stick This is barmy this, tha knows, Larry? It's been nearly two hours now! I mean fifteen minutes' grace you said. Everybody's turned up except them two silly sods!
Frank It's warm and all, isn't it?
Stick I don't know why they're all still sat on the coach, to be honest. You would have thought after two hours sat there in the heat that they'd have worked out that there's a problem, wouldn't you? Talk about thick!

Larry Well, they didn't expect anybody to go missing, did they?

Stick Have you seen 'em and all, just sat there looking out of the window. They look like they're fading.

Frank It is warm though, isn't it?

Stick It is on there. I haven't got the air conditioning on ... they must be cooking.

Larry has a look around the fourth wall

Larry Where the bloody hell are they?

Stick I bet it stinks on that bus!

Frank Do they know where we were waiting?

Larry Well, I let 'em off here and told them, but you know what this lot are like; two and two never makes bloody four, does it? They might have gone on a cruise for all I know!

Stick I told you, you wouldn't come back with a full load!

Larry Aren't we all right?

Stick Dropping like flies now!

Larry Aren't we all right?

Frank The way it's going you'll be going back with an empty coach.

Larry Aren't we all right?

Stick Hey, he'll like that, he can sing all he bloody wants then!

Frank He could leave the coach here and get a lift back with you!

Stick Ay, it'd cost him though, and there's definitely no singing on mine. Especially Mario Lanza...

Larry Tha wouldn't know a good song if it bit thee arse!

Stick I don't know that one, how does it go?

Frank This is getting beyond a joke now.

Stick It was getting beyond a joke at Leicester Forrest; she got on the Disneyland bus then, maybe she's started walking back home to get to the funeral?

Frank Oh, don't...

Stick Maybe they've collapsed somewhere ... didn't look too well, did they?

Frank None of 'em did this morning!

Stick They won't look well after they've been sat inside for two hours ... they must be dripping wet through!

Frank Put the air conditioning on.

Stick No, sod 'em!

Frank Stick!

Stick Have you got yours on?

Frank No!

Stick Well then, leave 'em, they're nearly done now anyway!

Frank Go and put the air conditioning on!

Stick You haven't got yours on!

Frank We're parked in the shade.

Stick They'll be all right, just be lightly barbecued! Anyway, it's all diesel, isn't it? Dennis'll have a go at me if I keep re-filling it.

Frank They're going to be badly on that coach.

Stick They look badly already, if you ask me!

Larry Ay, Mack and Mabel looked dreadful at breakfast. Didn't have any sleep according to form! I told her to get some shut-eye on the run down here, but she can't relax on a bus she said.

Stick Well what's she bloody come for then? Isn't it completely unbelievable!

Larry She said she can't go on a plane, she can't go on a boat, and he can't drive because he's had a heart do...

Stick It just gets better, doesn't it?

Larry And she can't relax on a coach because she thinks there's going to be an accident!

Stick This is what I'm saying, it's like cuckoo's nest...

Larry She was playing bloody hell with her daughter on that mobile; she booked it for her and made her come!

Stick Well, that's bloody clever, what if she has a turn and we're left with her?

Frank That's why we're here!

Stick These trips, I tell you, nowt but hassle! Look at Johnny Mac...

Frank Oh, he's off again, look...

Stick He's got it sorted...

Frank If you're that desperate...

Stick I'm telling you; it's taken ten years off him doing them Spanish runs.

Frank Well, he looks older to me...

Stick At least he's got a bloody tan...

Frank He's all wrinkled though, isn't he, looks like a bloody handbag!

Stick I'm telling you, it's taken years off him.

Larry Well, tha knows what to do.

Stick I will and all. I mean it's not only all the driving; you've to play nursemaid and all.

Frank There's a load of trouble on them Spanish trips, you know?

Stick They should shoot this lot!

Larry I'll shoot these two when they bloody turn up!

Stick Well, if you're going to shoot 'em anyway, let's assume that they're not coming back and get these bloody wagons rolling, Larry. I mean come on; talk about "When it's summertime in Heidelberg"? It'll be sodding Autumn before we get there the way things are going!

Frank Where the bloody hell are they...?

Stick (*to the audience*) We waited another half hour in the sweltering heat, then Frank spotted them. Sissy and Doris! They were sat like two women

from them Beryl Cook drawings on the back of the Rudeshiem tourist train
... and they were going round for the tenth time having more cheese and
tomato sandwiches and the same conversation...

*Music. The Lights change. Larry becomes Doris. Frank becomes Sissy. They
sit on a case and face out to the audience*

Sissy Bloody hell!
Doris Oh ay.
Sissy Poor Jean...
Doris Ay...
Sissy And all she wanted was a run out...
Doris Oh ay...
Sissy Just a run out...
Doris Oh ay...
Sissy It's not a lot to ask, is it?
Doris It's not, is it?
Sissy It's not a lot to ask!
Doris It's not, is it?
Sissy She would have loved this little train...
Doris She would...
Sissy I mean it doesn't seem right us still going to Heidelberg but...
Doris What can you do?
Sissy What can you do...
Doris I mean we can't just go back home...
Sissy We can't go back home, can we?
Doris No.
Sissy I mean, I think she'd've wanted us to still come but...

A beat

Doris Mind you, she could be a funny bugger could Jean!
Sissy She could...
Doris She could...
Sissy She could be a funny bugger.
Doris It's no use pretending any other, because she could be a funny bugger!
Sissy She could!
Doris I mean when Colin died, I took her some mince pies round, I didn't
ask for owt for 'em, but do you know, she never offered me owt?
Sissy No...
Doris She never offered me owt!
Sissy No.
Doris And yet her own daughter would go and see her from Leeds, and she
used to give her petrol money.

Sissy She never!
Doris She used to give her petrol money!
Sissy Hee dear...!
Doris And she'd give her own daughter petrol money for going to see her.
Sissy And she's a chiropodist!
Doris She is!

A beat

Sissy Oh ay, she could be a funny bugger could Jean.
Doris She could.
Sissy She could be a funny bugger.

A beat

Doris Anyway, she's gone to a better place.
Sissy She has...
Doris Gone to a better place!
Sissy I've got another cheese and tomato sandwich if you fancy one.
Doris Oh no, I...?
Sissy Don't you fancy one?
Doris No, I...
Sissy I mean we've a lot left...
Doris I'd better not, I mean I've had that sausage and that's upset me.
Sissy I told you not to have one.
Doris Best sausage I've ever had was Kenny Knowles, it was the only sausage I could take without it giving me indigestion.
Sissy Ay, she's gone to a better place has Jean!

A beat

Doris Do you think we should be going back?
Sissy What?
Doris I mean everybody'll be waiting, won't they? I mean we've been on this for three hours now, my legs are stiffening up! It's shaking me to bits, to be honest!
Sissy Oh, let 'em wait, Doris!
Doris I'm ready for getting off, to be honest, it's playing havoc with my back!
Sissy Let 'em wait.
Doris Well...
Sissy You still end up in the same place whether you rush or take it steady.
Doris Well ay...
Sissy We'll go round once more for Jean, shall we?

Doris Well ay, I'm happy enough, I'll go round once more for Jean!
Sissy Let 'em wait! We're going nowhere fast, are we?

Music. The Lights change. Doris becomes Larry and Sissy becomes Frank

Stick They apologised for being late, but they knew what they were doing.
  They don't fool me… If ever I get like that you can shoot me!
Frank He doesn't mean that!
Stick I do! If you ever see me sat on the back of a tourist train anywhere,
  having the same mindless conversation, going over the price of sausage
  and sucking my gums, no matter where I am, just come up and shoot me,
  because it'll mean I've lost my mind!
Frank He doesn't mean that!
Stick I bloody do!

*The Lights change. Stick, Larry and Frank become members of the trip and
sing forcefully. They are almost at Heidelberg*

They sing a couple of verses of "Ain't She Sweet"

The Lights change

Larry Heidelberg castle stands above the city. It's one of the most popular
  destinations in Germany by all accounts.
Frank You pick facts up over the years, what with going to the same place
  over and over again! They reckon that the oldest human bone in Europe
  was found near Heidelberg. So it's always been popular.
Stick Ay, with crinklies!
Frank They've also got the oldest university in Germany.
Stick They can stick it up their arse for me…
Frank He doesn't mean that!
Stick I do!
Frank And there's lots of students.
Stick Ay, but you never get to meet 'em; too busy shepherding these about.
Larry Mario didn't do the film of *The Student Prince*, as you know. A lot
  of people think it's because he was too fat and he was, he couldn't fit in one
  of our loos; but in fact he'd had a row with the director; walked off the set,
  and never went back. He didn't suffer fools didn't Mario. Anyway
  Edmund Purden did the Prince and they used Mario's voice for the singing.
  Died when he was thirty-eight! Bloody hell, eh? He takes some and he
  leaves others!
Stick Ay, he takes all the interesting ones and leaves all the boring sods!

During the following, Stick becomes Mollie, and Frank becomes Connie

Larry When we checked in at the hotel, Arsenic and Old Lace had a right pop at me about Stick; as if it was my fault?

Connie He's the worse driver we've ever been with!

Mollie I mean we were sat there for nearly three hours and not once did he offer to put the air conditioning on!

Connie There were people on that coach gasping for their breath...

Mollie I had hoped that the trip would be relaxing, but frankly when you're frying by the Rhine, gasping for your breath it's not easy to relax, we've had quite a year as it is!

Connie Just leave it, Mollie, because the whole trip is a nightmare.

Larry Well, I'm sorry you think that...

Mollie I did think we might come again ... but if we do we'll not come with Larards!

Larry Well, I'm sorry you feel like that like...

Mollie And to be absolutely honest, the rest of the people on the trip are vulgar and crude...

Connie Mollie!

Mollie No, it's no use: I've had about enough of you all! I mean you can't speak to anyone on the trip without them telling you about their water works or when they last had bowel surgery.

Connie Mollie?

Mollie I had thought we might meet someone and have some discussion about the German romantics and Wagner, but frankly we've been hard pushed to get past talking about Arthur Scargill and Marks and Spencer's remnants! And the language... I mean I'm not a prude but...

Larry You'll not want to come down to the Bier Keller when we go down, then? We usually get everybody together for a sing song on the first night in Heidelberg; shall I put you on the list or do you want to find some entertainment on your own?

The Lights change. Music: "The Drinking Song" from The Student Prince. *Larry, Stick and Frank move* DS. *Each has a special overhead spot. Music plays under*

Frank In the back room of *The Bull*, we usually get them sat at long wooden tables singing "Drink, drink, drink!" This is what they've come for!

Larry Suddenly they're all students. They're all at *Ruder's Inn*...

Stick They serve steak on a wooden platter, a stuffed potato in baco foil and some rancid sauerkraut. It's about as German as Chairman Mao but they lap it up...!

Larry Everybody has a good time, you should hear 'em!

Frank Next door in Sepp's place, an authentic student pub, real Heidelbergers have the real experience!

Larry But it doesn't matter to our lot, they're all Westphalians now!

Frank We usually stand at the bar, and watch them have too much!

Larry Marx Brothers went well over the top, I could have tipped that!

Frank Arsenic and Old Lace forced three steins down them, and were giddy all the way back!

Stick Sissy and Doris shared half a stein, and showed no remorse!

Larry Mack and Mabel had a lemonade each... Bloody hell, I could have wept for 'em!

Stick And Martin had a half of lager, his mam and dad's steak, and half the wooden platter it came on.

Frank Well, she was right about one thing!

Stick He *could* eat two pies more than a pig!

Music fades. The Lights go out on Stick and Frank

Stick exits and becomes Harry with cardigan and baseball hat

Larry It was that night that I got talking to Harry. We were outside in the High Street ... getting a breather; Dot was sat with Martin and May talking about the time Pontefract lake froze over and three people went through the ice and died. No wonder she felt badly...

The Lights change. We are outside. It is evening. Dappled gobo: slight German music swell then fade

Harry enters

Harry Cooler out here!

Larry Oh ay! She all right now?

Harry She didn't get much sleep last night!

Larry I don't think anybody did!

Harry She doesn't sleep most nights these days; but you know, it's with her being away from home! Keeps thinking she's going to be badly again! She's had a heart job only seven months ago!

Larry Ay, I've been there, with my dad!

Harry Bloody hell, eh?

Larry Not pleasant!

Harry Bloody miracle to me...

Larry They reckon they're ten a penny these days, don't they?

Harry They are when they're happening to somebody else.

Larry She's got a fresh start though, hasn't she? Got a new engine in, should run for years! She could go on hundreds of these trips, think of the future ... there's so much out there, tha knows?

Harry She had to wait two years for it though…

Larry I love a success story though, don't you?

Harry They need 'em, don't they: NHS!

Larry Well, they did all right for me like…

Harry Ay?

Larry I had blood clots; eight years ago… Long distance run from Italy. Put me out for a year! They're fashionable now! Nobody had heard of 'em when I had 'em!

Harry Have to be careful, won't you, on a job like this?

Larry Well, this is my last run! Quit while I'm ahead I thought. Apparently they can develop at any time, so. I've dreamed of nowt but bloody motorways this last ten year, I can tell you!

Harry Well, I worked at Barnborough Pit, I dreamed of coal for twenty years!

Larry I hit some water last month, nearly lost it…

Harry They're big buses and all, aren't they?

Larry Black ice nearly put me off the road in early March. I feel like my luck's running out!

Harry You'd get on with our lass you, she feels the same!

Larry She'll be all right! She can do owt after what she's been through, can't she?

Harry Tha reckon?

Larry Oh ay!

Harry Did your dad?

Larry It was too late for my dad like … but…

A beat

Harry Anyway, you don't want to be hearing my woes, do you? I'd better go back in there and see what she's up to. If I'm long-winded she sets off in a panic, and that doesn't do her any good. And then *she* gets shouting, and that doesn't do me any good.

Larry Sounds like you're made for each other.

Harry Ay, we've always argued! I used to say to our Janice; in a relationship where there are no arguments, somebody is getting too much of their own way…

Larry Ay, it's true enough is that.

Harry I hope we can get her a good seat for the show tomorrow, or that'll be another problem. If I don't, I know what she'll say: fancy coming all this way and not getting a good seat!

Harry disappears us. *The Lights change. Frank comes into the scene with Larry*

Frank Not long now!

Larry Another night here and one in Brussels and that's me done.

Frank Bloody flies, doesn't it?

Larry Oh, don't!

Frank I mean I can remember when I started like it was yesterday, and when was that?

Larry Six years ago...

Frank Six years!

Larry To this week!

Frank Ay, it was. Have you been keeping a record?

Larry You just remember some things, don't you? *Student Prince* tomorrow, are you going?

Frank It's not my thing really.

Larry No?

Frank Not really.

Larry Have you seen it ever?

Frank Ay, I have: I bloody hated it. Too soppy for me! Not enough pain in it!

Larry Well, it gets to me.

Frank Well, you're a softy though, aren't you? You are, you know, really!

Larry Well, if you, you know, fancied going to see it, you know, just let me know.

Frank It's not really my thing.

Larry Thought it might be nice, to go for a meal afterwards, you know...

Frank Well...?

Larry You know ... for old times' sake...

Frank What?

Larry Well...

Frank Larry?

Larry What?

Frank Larry?

Larry What's up?

A beat

Frank Are you trying to chat me up?

Larry Who?

Frank You?

Larry I just thought it might be nice to, you know...

Frank You are, aren't you?

Silence

Larry Forget it, because it's just...

Frank You are, aren't you?

Larry Hey, I'm out of practice here, help me out...

Frank Larry?

Larry Bloody hell...

Frank Larry?

Larry What am I playing at?

Frank I don't know if I should feel flattered or what?

Larry Just forget it...

Frank Bloody hell, mate...

Larry Hey look, all right, I've dropped a bollock; wrong time, wrong place, wrong person; story of my bloody life!

Frank Well, you've took your time, haven't you? What is it, a final fling, I'll have a go at Frankie, she might think it's charity week?

Larry That's not fair!

Frank Bloody hell, Larry, I thought you were different.

Larry Ay, I thought I was!

Frank I thought we were mates?

Larry You're right, we are! I shouldn't have mentioned it. I feel a right pillock now. But I had to have a go, hell fire...

A beat

Frank Well, it's taken you long enough, hasn't it?

Larry I know, I'm a bit slow on the uptake. I've seen the other blokes at the depot fussing all over you. And I didn't want to be part of that setup...

Frank Well, I am flattered, I tell you...

Larry Don't make fun...

Frank I'm not. At least you're a bloody gentleman; but waiting six years is a bit extreme...

Larry Forget it. It's pointless anyway, I've had a drink, I always talk blob when I've had a drink!

Frank I mean you're not like Johnny Mac!

Larry I know that.

Frank He didn't mess about!

Larry Eh?

Frank He tried it on with me the first week I was there.

Larry He would do...

Frank Anyway that was a mistake... I shouldn't have done owt with him but you learn, don't you?

Larry Johnny Mac?

Frank Ay, I know, isn't it pathetic?

Larry He's an arsehole...

Frank He is, but he's got such a nice arsehole and all.

Frank disappears US. *Larry remains suspended in disappointment*

Larry He might have, but it's never done owt for me!

Music: Gaudeamus Igitur. *The Lights change. Stick comes* DS *and picks up the narrative*

Stick The next night we drove all our sad cases up to Heidelberg Castle to see a group of enthusiastic amateurs slaughter *The Student Prince.* I mean it's bollocks to me but I'd never seen a production like this...
Frank Larry had made sure that Mack and Mabel got seats right near the front.
Stick Ay, and just to ensure they had a good time he sat between them... That's one of the troubles with Larry, he gets bloody carried away!

Stick becomes Harry, Frank becomes Dot. They find seats on a case, watching the show, which is in the fourth wall. Larry comes and sits beside them. They watch the play with interest

Larry Are you enjoying it?
Dot Sshh...
Larry Are we close enough for you...
Harry Sssh!
Larry Need bloody fish eyes sitting this close, don't you?
Dot Ssshhh!
Larry Are you warm enough?
Dot Sssh!
Larry I hope there's no loud bangs or owt...
Harry Ssshhh...!
Larry Oh, this is a good bit, I melt at this bit...

Music: "Summertime in Heidelberg" plays. It is clear that Dot and Harry are enjoying the singing as the opening refrain of the song starts, but as the Mario Lanza part is reached in the song, Larry can't help but join in the lyrics, killing it for Dot, Harry and the entire audience. As he sings, Dot and Harry try to shut him up, to no effect. Larry sings a verse of the song

The music continues playing, but softer. Stick comes DS *as himself, Dot becomes Frank*

Stick I couldn't bloody believe it! The silly sod was only stood up singing along for the rest of the show.
Frank Everybody was gob-smacked, especially the cast... And the thing was, Larry was better than any of them...

Larry I couldn't help it! I was there, do you know I mean? I was in Heidelberg, I was at *Ruder's Inn*, and it was my last night!

Frank And the funny thing was Mack and Mabel stood up and sang along with him, talk about laugh; the three of them were singing along like they'd just escaped from somewhere not right!

Stick And at the end, to cap it all, bloody Larry gets Mack and Mabel on stage with the rest of the cast to take a bow.

Frank And before you knew it everybody in the audience and on stage were applauding them!

Stick It was cuckoo's nest... I swear it... He should be locked up!

Larry I just felt so bloody happy for 'em, that they'd made it, I wanted to get them back to the hotel after the show, but they were having none of that, they were up for a night on the town!

During the following, Stick and Larry move US

Stick I'll never forget that night. We took all three coaches back down to the city, parked up on Bismark-platz, and piled into this place called Gustav's House!

Frank I didn't know whether to laugh or cry when we got in there! They were all there. Sissy, Doris, Arsenic and Old Lace. The Marx Brothers, Mack and Mabel, they were all there; laughing, drinking, doing the bloody conga. And when Martin slipped four euros into a juke box and started dancing with Doris, I thought I'd lost my bloody mind!

Music: Model Kraftwerk. *Doris and Martin dance together. They are appalling, funny and touching, the effect should be unsettling and funny, bad dancing par excellence. Frank enters the dancing. As they dance badly, Martin's hat is taken off and he becomes Stick, Doris dances with Frank to become Sissy*

As the music fades and the Lights fade, Doris and Sissy sit with their luggage. It is the next morning and they are ready for home. Stick stands at the other side of the stage and watches them

Sissy Well, we're ready, aren't we?

Doris We are!

Sissy They said be early.

Doris They did!

Stick The next morning the Beverley Sisters sat waiting for their coach, an hour before anybody else. I just don't get these people!

Sissy Sad to be going back?

Doris Well, I've always found travelling much better than arriving.

Sissy Oh, I don't know about that, arriving was quite good when I was in my twenties.

Doris I never had much interest in it to be honest. A lot of pushing and pulling I always thought.

Sissy Mind you, they're all at it today, aren't they? Like bloody animals! They don't know each other two minutes and they're getting married. And then they're in *Hello*...

Doris They should make 'em stop together!

Sissy That's right.

Doris See how they like it.

Sissy No stomach for it.

Doris Not today.

Sissy I mean look at me! Forty-two years!

Doris Oh!

Sissy Forty-two years!

Doris I know.

Sissy Forty-two years!

Doris Forty-two years!

Sissy With the same man!

Doris Forty-two years!

Sissy With the same man.

Doris They don't want it today. It's too easy for 'em.

Sissy Forty-two years married to the same man, it's no wonder I strayed, you know, when I think about it!

Doris No!

Sissy And I'll tell you this. I never loved him like I should have.

Doris Forty-two years and all.

A beat

Sissy Bloody Jean, eh...?

Doris It makes you wonder what's round the corner, doesn't it?

The Lights change. Doris becomes Larry. Sissy becomes Frank. Stick comes DS and picks up the narrative

Stick Later that morning we pulled out of Heidelberg with *Golden Days* just a distant hum, thank God!

Frank No place looks good in the rain and the Rhine is no different. A wet road puts you on your toes, and it's a long haul back to Brussels...

Larry Ay, and it's uphill all the way!

Frank He always says that!

Stick We arrived at the Hotel Ibis at about six-ish.

Frank Unloaded everybody, pointed them in the direction of the Grand Place...

Stick And then we watched the sad sods waddle into the damp Belgian night looking for chocolates, truffles and *The Adventures of Tin Tin!*

Larry Mind you, the Marx brothers had another location in mind.

Stick Just past the station Midi is Brussels' red light district. It's a toilet compared to Hamburg and Amsterdam but...

Larry And he'd bloody know, wouldn't he?

Stick Everybody goes to look, there's all sorts of shows on. I think they're even doing *The Student Prince*, Larry!

Music. The Lights change. Larry becomes Wally, Stick becomes Brian and Frank becomes Len. They walk DS into three overhead spotlights. They don their flat caps. Wisps of smoke are caught in the spotlights

Brian Bloody hell, where are we?

Len By gum!

Wally All that meat and no veg, Len!

Len By gum.

Wally I said, all that meat and——

Len I heard you!

Brian What a bloody job, eh?

Len You wouldn't do that job like that, would you, Wally?

Wally I wouldn't!

Len Bloody stinks!

Wally There's dog mess, all over, I think I've stood in some.

Brian Can't you watch where you're going?

Wally It's all over the shop!

Len You're going to trail that back! And we're sharing again!

Brian Well, I think I've seen about enough!

Wally We've only just started!

Brian I'm better than this!

Wally Have you had enough?

Brian I'm not having any more of this, I mean I've got our lass badly at home with sugar and I'm down here in this?

Wally We're only looking.

Brian We're better than this, aren't we?

Len Oh, I think I've stood in sommat now!

Brian Well, you can please yourselves, but I'm better than this!

Len There's a bloke over there taking a dump, look!

Wally and Brian look out front. And speak together

All Bloody hell!

Wally Last time I saw that I was down Wath pit!

Brian Where's tha brought us, Wally?

Len This is supposed to be a bloody sophisticated city, this is!

Brian Well, if this is sophistication, they can stick it up their arses.

Wally I think some of 'em do!

Len I tell thee sommat, they call Cayton Bay and Brid, they call all the east coast of Yorkshire, but you don't get this there!

Wally Well, only on a good night, Len!

Brian I'm going, I'm not having this, you must think we're sodding desperate to bring us down here! Hell fire, I've more oil in my lamp than to hang about with this scum! I mean I know we're low, Wally, but bloody hell...

Brian departs from his spotlight

Len He's right!

Wally Ay, it's humanity with its pants down, isn't it?

Len Well, I don't know about thee, Wally, but it's not doing owt for me!

Wally No, I know what tha means!

Len Shall we get off?

Wally Let's just walk to the end, tha never knows we might see sommat a bit different...

Stick enters the spotlight, carrying Martin's bobble hat

Stick They walked all the way down that road looking for sommat different. When they got to the end, they saw sommat a bit different, they saw Martin. (*He puts Martin's bobble hat on and smiles*)

Len What you doing then, Martin?

Martin What are you doing?

Wally Just looking!

Martin What are you looking for?

Wally Same as thee probably!

Martin Oh, right!

Wally What's tha been playing at, Martin?

Martin I've been in twice!

Len Bloody hell!

Wally Tha never has, has tha?

Martin That one at end's good; she doing two for the price of one tonight ... so I went in twice...

Len What would thee mam say if we told her what tha's been doing though?

Wally She wouldn't be happy, would she?

Martin She'd never believe you though, would she...?

Martin smiles a huge smile, walks from his light and exits US

Music fades. The Lights change. Larry and Frank remain DS

Larry It's always the same in Brussels on the way back; somebody disappears up there for a sniff about. Sometimes we take trips. There was this one time we were driving down past all these women in their windows and I hears this old woman from Wakefield tell her mate, "Hairdressers are open late, look"... We were up and out early the next morning. Everybody wanted to get home now, especially us!

The Lights change. Frank and Larry begin to move the cases around. They are tired and don't have quite so much energy

Nearly there now, Frank!

Frank (*with the cases*) Are these getting heavier or is it me?

Larry Nearly all over, bar the shouting.

Frank At least you did your party piece.

Larry I still can't bloody believe I did that! Nobody's been able to look me in the eye since, they all think I'm crackers. I bloody might be for all I know. I mean I'm sorry about that other job and all, embarrassed my bloody self there, didn't I?

Frank Don't worry about it.

Larry Oh dear, Frank...

Frank What?

Larry I'm going to bloody miss you, lass.

Frank Don't be so soft...

Larry I mean you'll be stuck on here with that mad gett; I've always thought I was there for you, kind of thing.

Frank You didn't think that in Heidelberg, did you?

Larry That was bloody stupid, I've admitted that! I was just surprised about you and Johnny Mac. Surprised and disappointed if you want to know the truth.

Frank I'm only human, Larry.

Larry I am and all.

Frank Too late though.

Larry He's such a malignant twat is that Johnny Mac... I mean I know it's nowt to me, but since you told me I can't get the image of you and him rolling about on the back seat of a bloody new coach out of my head!

Frank It was six years ago! Come on, Larry, you've got a wife and you're retiring to be the Red Shadow; I mean get a grip!

Larry I always put you up there though.

Frank Oh, come on!

Larry I know it sounds daft but... Oh dear, Frankie lass, you've kept me going this last six year.

Frank What are you like, you silly old sod...?

Stick enters from US

Stick You rung the office this morning?

Larry Eh?

Stick Not rung up, have you?

Larry Not yet, why, what's the roads like?

Stick You haven't heard then?

Frank About what?

Stick Johnny Mac...

Larry Don't tell me owt else about that tosser and them young lasses, I'll pull my bloody hair out!

Stick Ay well, he's come off the road, hasn't he?

Frank What?

Stick There's three English kids critical apparently.

Larry Oh, bloody hell...

Stick He's all right like but...

Larry He bloody would be and all...

Stick You what?

Frank What's happened?

Stick Dennis doesn't know, he's come off into a field or sommat.

Larry Speeding, I bet he's bloody speeding, he's always going too bloody fast, that daft gett!

Frank Wow now, Larry, wow, steady on...

Larry They're only bits of kids and he's been driving like somebody bloody barmy, I bet you...

Frank Whoah, steady...

Larry He'll not be looking at 'em in the rear mirror now, will he?

Frank Whoah, Larry, whoah...

Stick You what?

Larry He was bloody asking for it...

Stick and Larry are beginning to get aggressive with each other

Stick How do you know?

Larry Should have kept his sodding eyes on the road, if you ask me...

Frank Whoah, whoah! Now, whoah!

Stick That's my mate...

Larry Bloody crackers...

Stick You what?

Larry You both are...

Frank Hey, hey, hey!

Stick You want to watch that bloody lip, Larry, or I'll shut it for you!

Larry Yeah?

Stick Yeah?

Larry Yeah?

Stick Yeah?

Larry Come on then, I'll wipe the bloody floor with thee...

Frank Hey now, hey now, hey, bloody hell...

Larry Come on, I'm a bloody old man and I'll lick thee... I wasn't in the bloody SAS for nowt, we used to eat twats like thee for sommat to do... Come on...

Stick Tha was never in the bloody SAS, you soft gett!

Larry Thee come and see if I wasn't. I've had about enough of thee on this trip, tha needs some bloody manners teaching, tha does!

Stick From thee, tha's farting every verse end!

Larry If tha doesn't like it on here, go and get yourself to Spain; drink yourself bloody senseless, you've not got far to go...

Frank Larry, leave it, calm down ... now hey...

Larry He's no sodding respect, he hasn't!

Frank Hey now, for God's sake give it a bloody rest or I'll sort the both of you out, SAS or no bloody SAS. I'll show you what a good hiding is if you don't give it a bloody miss. I was in the sodding Navy and that's a fact; now pack it in you soft getts! Both of you. Pack it in ... we've still a long way to go, if you want to fight, sort it out at the bloody depot, but not here!

Silence

There's been a bloody accident, there's no point us going off the deep end! What good is that going to do? Bloody cool it, hell fire, we've to go all the way back. Last thing we want is another one!

Larry You're right!

Stick He comes out with such wank, though.

Larry He's off again, look, can't keep it shut!

Stick It's a good job tha leaving, Larry, because tha's a bloody liability...

Larry Frank, he's off again!

Stick Johnny Mac would shit on thee as a driver...

Larry I'm as good a driver as anybody at Larards I'll tell thee that. In fact, I'll tell thee sommat else, Wallace Arnold's were after me two years ago, old cock!

Stick Ay, I know, but they didn't accept thee because tha's had blood clots, and tha's likely to have 'em again given what tha bloody eats.

Larry He's on about what I bloody eat now.

Frank Stick, leave it...

Stick And smoking'll not do thee any good!

Larry I'll do what I bloody want...

Frank Stick, that's enough now...

Stick And what about thee mental health? I mean come on, tha lives in a
bloody musical. Everybody at the depot thinks tha's crackers, and when
I tell 'em tha got up on stage at Heidelberg singing along they're going to
know tha's not a full shilling...

Larry I did that for Mack and Mabel, you sarcastic gett!

Stick Mack and Mabel, they're called Dot and Harold or sommat.

Larry He doesn't even know their bloody names, look!

Stick Neither do you, you make 'em up! I'll be glad when tha's gone, I will.
At least we'll have no more made-up names and singing.

Larry Anyway, tha knows blob about me and my bloody health!

Stick I do.

Larry You don't!

Frank Larry, leave it now...

Stick Well, tha's told me all about the blood clots and thee dad dying from
clots and how it runs in the family before, or have you forgotten what
you've bloody said? Silly sod! We're lucky we get to where we're going
with him leading us, because he can't remember what he's said and what
he hasn't! Can tha?

Larry I can't remember if I've told you or not, to be honest.

Stick See, see...!

Frank Bloody leave it now, for goodness sake ... you're like little kids, the
pair of you.

The Lights change. Stick, Larry and Frank begin to sing Show Me the Way
To Go Home

Frank takes up the story as she addresses the audience

Frank We pulled out of Brussels and it was still teaming it down. There was
an uneasy truce between Larry and Stick, and I think they'd taken me up
on my suggestion to sort it out at the depot. That'll be good, there's
supposed to be a surprise leaving "do" for Larry when we get back!

Stick We stopped off for the inevitable hypermarket quickie at the Chunnel,
and everybody bought countless cigs and bottles of wine. And before you
knew it we were back in Sheffield!

Larry We dropped Arsenic and Old Lace off near Jessops just so they didn't
get lost in their own city; you could tell they'd enjoyed Stick's company,
they tipped him all of three quid!

Frank Then we dropped in Ponte. Martin and his mam and dad tipped Larry three quid and all, between them. And when he got off, Martin had a smile on his face a mile wide! But that was nothing to do with the tip.

Stick Mack and Mabel got off without tipping at all. I thought that was just classic. They'd had enough of him, and who could blame them; after all, he'd ruined their night!

Larry Now that's not true... You see, they were good people. They didn't make a show of giving me owt, like some do. In fact Harry slipped me twenty-five quid around the back of the bus and thanked me for being there for 'em! It was him that made me think: I like these folk, what am I packing it in for... They need me...

Frank What about your health?

Larry Twenty-five quid, hell fire, it was what they got a week from t' bloody Social more or less!

Frank Anyway, we let the Marx brothers off at Doncaster Arndale.

Music. The Lights change. Larry becomes Wally. Frank becomes Len, Stick becomes Brian

Brian Oh, I'm stiff. Bloody hell. That's a journey, isn't it?

Len That is a bloody journey.

Wally He should've come up the A1, he'd have been better with that, it's twenty miles nearer.

Brian So are we going on another one or not?

Wally Well, I'm go on one, but I'm not sharing a room again, I mean that was just bloody ridiculous.

Len Well, I'll go on another one, but I'm not going if Wally's going to keep laying the bloody law down! If it's not one thing, it's another.

Brian Well, I agree with that!

Len It's been bloody non-stop and my nerves just can't stand it! I mean I've had all about the low interest rates for the last three hours. I know all about low interest rates. That's why we're on a bloody bus trip. We can't afford owt else. I put a lump sum away and it's making nowt...

Brian Well, tha does go on, Wally...

Wally Well, I'm sorry if I go on, but it's like I say; you've both got somebody to talk to when you're get home. I've got nobody! When I get in the house I just sit and look at the bloody fire. That's why I might go on, I don't mean owt by it. I'm just pleased to talk to somebody...

Music underscores. The Lights change. Larry becomes Doris and Frank becomes Sissy. They make an effort to get some cases together. They stand where we picked them up. Stick watches as he delivers some cases to them

Sissy That's that then, Doris.

Doris That's that then.

Sissy Another one over.

Doris Ay, we can say we've done that now.

Sissy And I didn't get a bloody cuckoo clock. You know what that means, don't you?

Doris No.

Sissy I'm going to have to go again, aren't I?

Doris Well, I'll come with you if you want!

Sissy I'm a lot better when I'm going somewhere than I am at home, Doris. I like to be going somewhere. It's a lot better going somewhere when you're seventy-nine than going nowhere.

Doris It is and all, ay…!

Sissy Now then, I've just thought on…

Doris What's up?

Sissy How are we going to get home…?

Music. The Lights change. Doris and Sissy take off their headscarves slowly, to reveal Larry and Frank. Stick joins them. We are now back at the start of their mystery trip journey. They begin to move the cases

Larry Ay, it was a good trip was that, there were some nice people on that trip!

Stick Bloody complainers all of 'em…

Larry I did some thinking on that trip!

Stick Makes a change then!

Frank I called that the Johnny Mac trip…

Larry Oh ay…

Frank He couldn't stop going on about Johnny Mac, could you?

Larry He was bloody lucky with them kids…

Frank He was and all…

Larry He was lucky they pulled through!

Stick I tell you sommat, it's always a relief to me when these crinkly trips are over.

Frank It is to everybody!

Stick I mean if somebody doesn't drop dead, at the very least they come back with a case of the screaming squits!

Frank That's what being alive is like over the age of fifty-eight, isn't it, Larry?

Larry Ay, it's all waiting for thee, Stick lad, it's just round the corner.

Stick Ay well, after this mystery trip I'm on a Spanish run! Dennis wants me to shotgun Johnny Mac… Oohh, I can't wait… Tossa De Mar. Oh oh!

Larry Tha'll be a proper tosser then!

Stick That's right!

Larry Not just an apprentice.

Stick That'll keep me young. It's taken ten years off Johnny!

Larry It'll get thee in the end though!

Stick No, it wain't...

Larry And when old age creeps up on thee I hope it ravages thee, and tha's the most miserable, aching, crippled bastard to ever walk a pair of shoes.

Stick That's what I like about Larry, never uses one word when forty will do!

Larry And that's what I like about thee and all!

Stick What?

Larry Nowt!

Stick Well, tha's taken thee time saying it!

Larry Ay, but I take my time tha sees coz I knew I'd get there in the end!

Stick Go on, you silly old gett!

Larry Nearly there, Frank... (*He hauls some cases and carries them* US *to the exit*) Nearly there...

Larry exits

Stick hauls a number of cases and turns to Frank

Stick They should shoot 'em when they get like that, tha knows?

Frank You'd need a bloody elephant gun for Larry though, wouldn't you! According to form he was in the SAS, Mad Jack served wi' him, so you were lucky in Brussels!

Stick I thought he was retiring, what happened to all that?

Frank He told Dennis that he wanted to stay on, said he loved it! Couldn't live without it he said. Loves the people is what he told me!

Stick He's bloody crackers... (*He struggles to pick up a case*) What have they got in here? (*He struggles with some cases and goes* US) Bastards!

Stick exits

Frank picks up some cases and turns to leave, then addressses the audience

Frank Mystery trips! You'd think they were going round the world. Look at this lot! It's only a one nighter in Scarborough! Everybody on the coach knows that...

Larry enters and picks up some more cases

Larry Nearly there...

Frank I mean that's not much of a mystery, is it?

Stick enters and collects some more cases

Larry Just seen them two from Beverley, Stick. The Beverley Sisters, Sissy
and Doris...

Stick They're not coming on this one, are they?

Larry Ay, I'll put 'em on your coach, shall I? I know tha likes a sing song!
(*He collects some more cases*) Nearly there...

As Larry exits, Stick picks up some more cases

Stick Bastards...

Stick carries his cases and exits

Frank You know what'll it be like, don't you? Bloody chaos! I hope nobody
dies! But Larry's there, in't he? And you know Larry, he'll have Mario
Lanza playing all the way up to Scarborough, he'll get 'em all singing, and
if they cause any trouble in the shoe shops there's an ex-SAS man there for
'em. I mean it's like he says, when you're nearly sixty there's so much to
look forward to, isn't there...?

Music: Mario Lanza singing Donkey Serenade. *Frank starts to move some
cases*

Larry enters singing to the music

Stick drags himself back on stage

*As the Lights fade, the music swells and Larry continues to sing like Mario
Lanza to the vast annoyance of Stick and the delight of Frank*

CURTAIN

FURNITURE AND PROPERTY LIST

Further dressing may be added at the director's discretion

ACT I

On stage: Flat with image suggesting skyline
Faded route map of Europe
Suitcases
Overcoats
3 headscarves
3 handbags
3 flat caps
Baseball cap with "San Francisco" inscribed
Spectacles
2 smart hats
Beer
Radio

Off stage: 2 large cases (**Frank**)
2 cases (**Stick**)
2 cases, bag (**Larry**)
Cases (**Stick**)
2 cases (**Larry**)
Cases (**Frank**)
Glass of hot milk (**Harry**)
Suitcases (**Frank**)

Personal: **Sissy:** lit cigarette
Larry: cigarettes, lighter (carried throughout)
Sissy: lit cigarette

ACT II

On stage: As before

LIGHTING PLOT

Property fittings required: nil
Box set. The same throughout

ACT I

To open: Overall general lighting

Cue 1	Musical sting *Change lights to slight focus* DS	(Page 4)
Cue 2	Musical sting *Overall general lighting*	(Page 6)
Cue 3	Musical sting *Fade lights to focus in another area*	(Page 6)
Cue 4	**Wally**: "…interest rates low like that!" *Change lights*	(Page 7)
Cue 5	**Stick**: "…his anorak didn't convince me!" *Change lights*	(Page 7)
Cue 6	**Larry**: "…he never gave her roses…" *Change lights*	(Page 8)
Cue 7	**Dot**: "…it would come to this but…" *Change lights*	(Page 9)
Cue 8	**Larry**: "…if the singing starts early!" *Change lights, tighter light on* **Larry**, **Stick** *and* **Frank**	(Page 10)
Cue 9	**All**: "…down Paradise Road" *Change lights*	(Page 10)
Cue 10	**All**: "And I was the only boy…" *Change lights, spotlight on* **Stick**	(Page 11)

Cue 11	**Larry**: "Nearly there…"	(Page 12)
	Change lights	
Cue 12	**Sissy**: "…all sharing the same bedroom."	(Page 14)
	Change lights, window gobo DS *from "fourth wall"*	
Cue 13	**Wally**: "…if you keep doing that, sunshine!"	(Page 15)
	Change lights	
Cue 14	**Larry**: "…but I never bloody win owt!"	(Page 16)
	Change lights, spotlight C *for* **Dolly**	
Cue 15	**Dolly**: "…have a great holiday, won't you…"	(Page 18)
	Change lights	
Cue 16	**Stick**: "…they're a liability that lot!"	(Page 18)
	Change lights	
Cue 17	**Stick**: "…arrived in Boppard about two-ish!"	(Page 21)
	Change lights	
Cue 18	**Stick**: "…who looks the most frightening?"	(Page 22)
	Change lights	
Cue 19	**Frank**: "…that was the end of it!"	(Page 24)
	Change lights, room gobos	
Cue 20	**Len**: "…wouldn't have done it like that…!""	(Page 24)
	Change lights	
Cue 21	**Stick**: "I wouldn't have played it like that!"	(Page 25)
	Change lights, gobos suggesting balmy September evening	
Cue 22	**Stick** exits	(Page 28)
	Slowly bring up spotlight on **Larry**	
Cue 23	**Larry**: "…looking through the window…"	(Page 28)
	Change lights	
Cue 24	**Dot**: "In the middle of bloody nowhere?"	(Page 29)
	Change lights, spotlight on **Larry**, *fade light on* **Dot** *and* **Harry**	
Cue 25	**Larry**: "…Red Shadow to be back on the road…"	(Page 30)
	Start slow fade of lights	

Cue 26   **All** dump luggage back on stage   (Page 30)
              Fade lights to black

ACT II

To open: Overall general lighting

Cue 27   **All** are waiting, sitting on suitcases   (Page 31)
              Change lights

Cue 28   **Frank**: "...in the distance coming down..."   (Page 34)
              Change lights

Cue 29   **Len**: "...would tha, Brian?"   (Page 35)
              Change lights

Cue 30   **Stick**: "...and the same conversation..."   (Page 38)
              Change lights

Cue 31   **Sissy**: "...nowhere fast, are we?"   (Page 40)
              Change lights

Cue 32   **Stick**: "I bloody do!"   (Page 40)
              Change lights

Cue 33   **All**: "Ain't she sweet?"   (Page 40)
              Change lights

Cue 34   **Larry**: "...some entertainment on your own?"   (Page 41)
              Change lights, special overhead spots on **Larry**,
                  Stick *and* **Frank**

Cue 35   **Stick**: "...two pies more than a pig!"   (Page 42)
              Fade lights on **Stick** *and* **Frank**

Cue 36   **Larry**: "No wonder she felt badly..."   (Page 42)
              Change lights, dappled gobo suggesting outdoor evening

Cue 37   **Harry** disappears us   (Page 43)
              Change lights

Cue 38   **Larry**: "...never done owt for me!"   (Page 46)
              Change lights

EFFECTS PLOT

ACT I

ACT II

Cue 27	**Larry**: "…No wonder she felt badly…" *Slight German music swell then fade*	(Page 42)
Cue 28	**Larry**: "…never done owt for me!" *Music:* Gaudeamus Igitur	(Page 46)
Cue 29	**Larry**: "I melt at this bit…" *Music:* Summertime in Heidelberg	(Page 46)
Cue 30	**Larry** ends singing a verse of the song *The music continues playing, but softer*	(Page 46)
Cue 31	**Frank**: "…I'd lost my bloody mind!" *Music:* Model Kraftwerk	(Page 47)
Cue 32	**Doris** dances with **Frank** to become **Sissy** *Fade music*	(Page 47)
Cue 33	**Stick**: "…doing *The Student Prince*, Larry!" *Music, when **All** in position* DS, *wispy smoke effect*	(Page 49)
Cue 34	**Martin** exits *Fade music*	(Page 51)
Cue 35	**Frank**: "…off at Doncaster Arndale." *Music*	(Page 55)
Cue 36	**Wally**: "…I'm just pleased to talk to somebody…" *Music underscoring*	(Page 55)
Cue 37	**Sissy**: "How are we going to get home…?" *Music*	(Page 56)
Cue 38	**Frank**: "…look forward to, isn't there…?" *Music: Mario Lanza singing* Donkey Serenade	(Page 58)
Cue 39	**Stick** drags himself back on stage *Swell music*	(Page 58)